FOOD AND FABLES
FRANCE

A unique book containing world class French recipes written in simple, easy to follow steps accompanied by an interesting fact or fable. Impress your guests by serving wine matched to each recipe by a sommelier.

The first book of a series including a region, its food and stories

Food and Fables

Copyright © 2008 by Food and Fables
Photographs © 2008 by Food and Fables

Inquiries should be addressed to: Customerservice@foodandfables.com
www.foodandfables.com

Cataloging-in-Publication Data
Beveridge, Brian; Philippon, Jean
Food and Fables, France

1. Cookery, French 2. Fables, French
i) Beveridge, Brian ii) Philippon, Jean iii) Title: Food and Fables
ISBN: 978-0-9820665-0-8 (English version)
TX719.373 2008   641 5944   LCCN#: 2008907578

Recipes and Culinary Expert: Chef Jean Philippon;
Photography, Writing, and Concept: Brian Beveridge;
Please contact us via the Food and Fables website

Printed in China by Hung Hing Off-Set Printing Co.

FOOD AND FABLES FRANCE

Thanks to the many, many people who helped make the completion of this book possible. For several years the book was 'almost' finished and it's nice to finally be done. Thanks to Chef Philippon for his fine culinary skills and perseverance in working with me in this endeavour over all these years; Jamie and really all of my friends who helped with their energy, enthusiasm, or expertise to get this book to where it is and ready for you. Also a quick thanks to John Loofs, sommelier, for providing the wine recommendations. It has been an incredible experience seeing how much people are willing to go out of their way to help someone accomplish a goal. It's also great to see how talented and knowledgeable my friends all are!

An interesting path was taken to get to the creation of this book that includes too many numerous chance encounters to mention here and what some would call fate. If we ever get the chance to meet please ask me about them. What did ultimately happen is that a novice cook / business major ended up working with an accomplished chef and teacher to write a book. Please take the time to read the short biography of the Chef as it is not often you find someone with his background, or someone who chose to physically walk around the country of France just for the experience.

The nice part for you in the partnership that worked on this book is that you will see many of the advanced recipes written from the perspective of a novice in an instructional manner, some of the pictures even from a classroom! Regardless of the outcome of your recipe, you should enjoy the interesting stories that accompany each dish. We truly hope you enjoy this book.

Thanks!

Brian & Jean

ABOUT CHEF J. PHILIPPON

While the food Chef Philippon creates will impress you, the story of his past will probably amaze you. Jean has accomplished what most people hope to in a lifetime. Born in Bordeaux, France he has traveled through the best kitchens in France working alongside greats such as Paul Bocuse and Joel Robuchon to learn his trade.

Through Jean's talents and travels he has become one of the presidents of the "Les Compagnons du Devoir" organization 15 000+ members strong. Jean became a president by no minor feat. To even become a member of this prestigious organization, rich in history, one must travel, work and learn from different compagnon individuals in the different areas of France. This event is called the "Tour de France". Jean completed his "Tour de France" in 1992 taking a total of 10 years to go and work from town to town throughout France. This 10 year mission was enough for Jean to be a 'compagnon', however for Jean, it was not enough. Jean wanted to learn what it was really like when the elder members in his organization were young, back when there were no cars, public transportation, or the conveniences we have today. When these elder members did their "Tour de France" 70+ years ago they had to go by foot, or potentially by horse, so Jean set off to do a new "Tour de France", this time by foot. In 1992, Jean started his walk, departing from Lausanne, Switzerland to Geneva, to Lyon, Nice, Cannes, Toulouse, Brive, Angouleme, Nantes, Rennes, Normandie, Paris, Tours, Burgandy, Neuchatel, and back to Lausanne taking 5 years to complete.

Currently an instructor at the L'institut Paul Bocuse in Lyon, France, Jean has won many awards in cuisine including the chevalier du mérite agricole medal, medals for the cities of Marseilles and Aix, plus many others.

* The compagnon organization is comprised of 3 main groups, l'Association ouvriére des Compagnon du Devoir, la fédération co-pagnonnique des Métiers du Batiment, and l'Union compagnonnique des Compagnons, of which Jean is a president and member.

TABLE OF CONTENTS

EFFECTIVE USE OF THE BOOK

Pages are designed to quickly give you the most information possible to make you successful.

The most important thing you need to know about recipes, is that any recipe is merely a guide. With each recipe you don't need to use every ingredient listed, or work at the precise temperature noted. In fact, some ingredients may not be available at your local grocery store! If you don't have one of the ingredients listed, try it without that ingredient or add something new, use your judgement. Maybe you will like your new recipe better than the original. Each new recipe is developed from experimentation and using different ingredients, cooked properly, changes only the taste, for better or worse. "A chef isn't a true chef until he can do more than follow someone else's set of instructions".

It is important to note that the only thing consistent with ovens and stoves is that the temperatures they function at are inconsistent. Knowing 'when' what you are cooking is ready is much more important than waiting the mandatory 15 minutes the recipe asks of you. While you may not get this 'feel' right the first few times, you will continue to improve.

Page Design

The recipe steps are meant to be concise and designed to help you prepare the dish in the best way possible. We have tried to leave some blank space beside these recipe steps so that you can document your own ideas, or make your own notes, as you make your recipes. For example, you may want to include a note about an ingredient you tried that worked out great or a little reminder for you on what is important to know or watch for at a critical step.

Before you get started with the recipe you should prepare your "mise en place" which is found right at the top of the page. We call this the 'mise en place' because it tells you what ingredients you need, the quantity required, and how to cut them before starting to cook. The quantities are of course based on personal consumption and preferences so this is a guideline only. Please note that the recipes assume you have water, butter, salt and pepper available in nominal amounts. We will only specifically mention them or the quantities for these ingredients if the recipe requires a specific amount or a special type.

The book also includes 'Tips and Tricks' which contain various pieces of helpful information. Some tips highlight the most important steps you'll need to be mindful of in the recipe, others are good ideas for substitutions, and other ideas are for good presentation of your dish. These tips should help you win every time!

Right at the top of the page you will see some quick facts to help you decide which recipe you are going to make. These quick facts are recipe difficulty, preparation time and cooking time, number of servings and a wine recommendation.

- **RECIPE DIFFICULTY** is a novel approach to help you decide which dishes you want to try given the time, ambition, and skills you have. It is important to note that this is a guideline as you can change the difficulty level merely by purchasing a filet, instead of removing the bones yourself. Also note, if you are a beginner they are probably all a little hard, and if you are an experienced chef, they are probably all easy! Please read the difficulty level descriptions found later in the introduction section of this book.

- **PREP TIME** is an estimate of how long it takes to get your 'mise en place' ready. 'Mise en place' means all of your ingredients listed are cleaned, cut, weighed, and ready to use. You can use this information as a shopping list and guide when deciding what recipes to make.

- **COOK TIME** is an estimate of the time it will take for you to take the recipe from mise en place stage to the finish. These times are impossible to predict accurately as they vary greatly from individual to individual and dish to dish. It should help function as a guide for you and help you choose which recipe to make.

- **SERVINGS** are an estimate based on average consumption, you will need to adjust based on your specific requirements.

- **WINE RECOMMENDATIONS** to enjoy with the meal were provided courtesy of sommelier John Loofs. We have listed a French label that you should be able to find at a local wine store, however, knowing that it may not always be possible to find this particular type of wine you will also see we have provided a grape varietal just in case. Its hard to go too far wrong with wine so feel free to ask your local store for advice as it will most likely be great as well. We think you will enjoy experimenting with the different varieties of wine with each recipe!

For most recipes you will find a picture of the finished dish with an example of a good presentation. Take note of some of the small techniques they use in the pictures to present the meal in a beautiful way, and then try some yourself. If you don't have the time or inclination to do an elaborate presentation it is not a problem. What's important is that you like to eat what you have made. In other instances, where appropriate, we have provided pictures of intermediate steps meant to be more instructional or informational.

Finally, you will find an interesting fact, story, myth, or legend about the recipe or the ingredients within. We find many of these fables fascinating and believe your guests will too when you share them. Why not impress them, not only with your food, but your stories as well!

BON APPETIT!

"A chef isn't a true chef until he can do more than follow someone else's set of instructions"

BOOK DESIGN AND LAYOUT

This book has been designed to help you entertain by providing great stories and delicious recipes, however, it's often the people and the event that make it really special. To help achieve that goal, we have included a special chapter on menu design. There you will find how to put together a nice menu, including examples of menus you may want to serve at various occasions:

Birthday's	Entertaining
Valentine's Day	Easter
Christmas	New Year's

Please see the section entitled "Menu Design" for all the details. Note the order of recipes in the book match that of the traditional order used in a menu. So as long as you serve dishes from the start of the book at the start of the meal, and work your way towards the end of the book in that order, you will do well.

COOK TIME, QUANTITIES, ADJUSTMENTS

The cooking times that we have provided are estimates to give you a rough idea of when the dish should be ready. Each oven and stove operates in its own way and in fact, the actual pots and pans that you use change the time and the temperature needed to cook! The best material to use for your pots or pans is copper, however some people find it expensive.

When you begin cooking you will start to develop the feel for when something is ready. Throughout the book, we have tried to include descriptions of when something is ready so that you have the best chance to win.

Quantities work a little the same way. The quantities used for one dish may or may not be enough for you. If this is the case, merely scale up the entire recipe by equal amounts. The same applies if you want to make for 6 and the suggested servings are for 4. A further adjustment you may need to make will depend on where you live and where you shop. For example, did you know that water boils at different temperatures based upon altitude? How about there are 45%, 55% and 65% flour? Therefore, a combination of factors will change the end result of your dish, perhaps not by much but it will have an affect. As you make a recipe and notice some of these factors make notes in the spaces provided – it's why we put those spaces there!

Serving Size 1	Serving Size 2	Serving Size 4	Serving Size 6
Carrots ½ lb	Carrots 1 lb	Mussels 100g	Mussels 150g
2 Onions	4 Onions	2 Onions	3 Onions
Cream 50ml	Cream 100ml	Butter 50g	Butter 75g

e.g multiply the carrots ½ lb by new serving size divided by previous 2/1 = 1lb

multiply 100g mussels by new serving size divided by previous 6/4 = 150g

THE INGREDIENTS

Ingredient lists are provided as a guide, however we do not mention butter, salt or pepper specifically in each recipe. We mention these ingredients only if there is a special kind or specific amount required. Much like water, it is expected that you have nominal amounts of these ingredients around.

No recipe is going to be perfect, nor does it need to be. It should be noted though that weighing ingredients is the most accurate approach, including for liquids. This is most important in baking and less important for other cooking. In making this book we recognized that for most people this isn't practical, so we have converted from measured quantities to measurements in easier quantities for you to find and use. You will find the conversions used at the end of the book, if you want to be more precise convert back into grams for all as that was the original base quantity of the recipe. Note "~" means approximately e.g. a recipe may call for 500 grams of meat which we have listed as ~1lb as it means about 1lb, in this case actually 1.1 lbs.

For the other ingredients don't be scared to deviate a little! Substitutions are a normal part of any kitchen and should be taken in stride. While the end taste of the recipe will undoubtedly change, sometimes that's good. Not having one ingredient is absolutely no reason not to make the dish! Even if the dish calls for beef and you use lamb, it's ok. Usually it is not a problem to substitute a bird of one type for another, or one meat for another, the only change you need to make is to consult the cooking temperature chart to ensure you have cooked the new meat to the right temperature. If you don't have chicken stock it is ok to add a little water instead. While the taste will not be as strong the recipe will still taste great.

New recipes, good recipes, come only from a 'chef' being creative and trying something new. It's why we have tried to leave as much blank space as possible on the pages so that you can make your own notes. Please write in new ingredients you like, tips that help you "win" or other ideas you may have. It's your book, so let's make it work for you.

We have attempted to classify the various recipes into the level of difficulty it will require to have a good end result. Each person will have different skills and ability, thus changing what is right for you. However, this should help guide your decisions on what to make.

DIFFICULTY LEVELS

LEVEL 1
Recipes that take the least amount of time to prepare Many mistakes will have a smaller impact on the end result. Least amount of difficult cuisine techniques involved

LEVEL 2
A mix of more advanced skills throughout the recipe

LEVEL 3
Requires more intensive concentration Recipes take more time to achieve desired end results. Advanced techniques that most likely require prior experience or having visually learned this technique previously

Tip - To put out an oil fire, cover the fire with a towel or another pot to remove oxygen and this will put out the fire. Do not use water to put out an oil fire. Another possibility is to throw baking soda on the fire.

Determining oil temperature
If you are not able to measure oil temperature you can use a toothpick to help you approximate. When the oil is at 355 °F (180 °C), and you place the toothpick in the oil, swarms of bubbles will raise up from the toothpick whereas at 210 °F (100 °C) only 1 or 2 bubbles will slowly rise to the top. Do not reuse toothpicks as they will not give consistent results.

Finally, you will find an interesting fact, story, myth, or legend about the recipe or the ingredients within. We find many of these fables fascinating and believe your guests will too when you share them. Why not impress them, not only with your food, but your stories as well!

MENU.

Childrens Birthday
Mini Pizza
Chicken 'en voile'
Cake and Ice Cream

Adults Birthday
Aperitif
Mini Quiche Lorraine & Leek Tarte
Beef w Green/Black Peppercorns
Vegetable then Cheese
Cake and Ice Cream & Coffee

For a Friend
Salmon Tartar with Cape
Gazpacho Soup
Minute Mushroom Chicken
Cheese
Crème Caramel & Coffee

Valentines Day
Fried Mussels with Tartar
Cream of Tomato soup
Duck a l'Orange
Rosti, then Cheese
Chocolate Mousse & Coffee

Christmas
Moules Mariniere
Beef Wellington
Gratin Dauphinois
Cheese
Crème Brule & Coffee
Macaroon

New Years Eve
Aperitif
Salmon Tartar with cape
Grilled Lobster
Trou Normand
Rosigny, then Cheese
Tarte Tatin & Coffee
Petit Four, then Champagne

MENU DESIGN

A menu is really a collection of plates that you plan to offer to your guests. Within a menu you can often find plates that contain "Wellington", "Marengo", or "Clamard". These names all have links to a historical event:

- Wellington is a Duke who fought against Napoleon
- Marengo is where Napoleon experienced a great victory as head of state
- Clamard is the name of the town where General De Gaulle was assassinated

When you use these or other names in a menu, be careful, as your guests could have strong feelings about these events. The menu and meal are designed to create a happy environment, facilitating communication, not creating bad feelings or memories. With this in mind, before deciding on the dishes in your menu, consider certain information about your guests such as taste, allergies, or ideals so that they will fully enjoy the experience.

All hosts enjoy impressing guests through their imagination and creativity when creating the menu. For example, one might try serving a red wine called St. Amour with a meal for Valentines Day, as "amour" means love in French.

The sections you find in this book are in order of how you would serve them to your guests. Generally the order to serve courses is:

Appetizer
Soup
Fish
Crustacean
Trou Normand
Bird/Fowl
Beef/Pork
Game
Cheese
Dessert

The list above is a menu you may find at an extravagant event, designed to serve many courses with small quantities of food. With this many courses the meal itself could take up to 5 hours to finish. In your home, when you decide what courses you are going to serve, remember the important part is to keep the order you find above, not the number of courses themselves. Generally, if you follow the order of courses above, you will enjoy your meal.

One thought in designing your menu is to always have thicker consistency dishes at the start of a meal, and lighter consistency dishes near the end. Using this technique allows people to finish everything you make for them and enjoy the meal. With a lighter consistency it is best to have a stronger taste, as this helps to compensate for the lighter texture.

Remember to use a variety of ingredients in the dishes you are making, unless that is, you are having fun for the night (i.e. dishes that all have chocolate in them). While we provide these guidelines it is also possible to change and use for example, mussels as a main course - merely change the quantity to reflect that of a main course instead of an appetizer.

The Lover of oysters | *Der Austernfreund*

COCKTAIL PARTY FOOD

A cocktail party is always a great time to enjoy many small hot and cold treats. First we will introduce you to some ideas for canapés, and later some warm dishes.

A canapé is a small piece of bread with different tastes on top. You can change any ingredient, and present the pieces any way you like, making the list of possibilities endless. We have provided nine basic ideas for you to start with and build upon. We have not given estimated times in this section as there is too much variation depending on the quantity you make and the tools you have. Instead we have used this space to give you more tips.

CANAPÉ

LETS GET STARTED...

A canapé is a small piece of bread with different tastes on top. You can change any ingredient, and present the pieces any way that you like, making the list of possibilities endless. For this reason, we have written 9 possibilities for you to try. The required time varies too much depending on the quantity you make and the tools you have to predict. Therefore, instead of estimates we have provided you more ideas and tips to use. A compound butter to add or complement the flavours can sometimes be very good, experimentation is encouraged.

1. Butter the slice of bread and layer pieces of salmon on top. Place wax paper on top (push a little to ensure it sticks). Carefully, turn over the bread with the salmon so that the wax paper is face down on the table. Now cut away the crusts and cut into smaller pieces. Cutting with the salmon against the table allows you to cut into smaller pieces without the difficulty normally encountered when cutting salmon directly. Cut in the form of an 'x' to make nice triangles later when you open. To decorate the top of these pieces take softened butter and put in a cornet. Squeeze quickly and the butter comes out in a very elegant, natural decoration. If you squeeze slowly, the butter will come out in straight normal lines that you have to arrange carefully. Remember that you need to decorate on either side of the line so that each piece is decorated.

2. Cut circles in bread using a circle shaped form and then toast. Only lightly toast, and then butter the bread, add a melon ball and wrap in meat. Add chives for height if you like.

3. Butter the slice of bread and layer meat of your choice on top.   Put wax paper on top of the meat and push it against the meat (a little) with your hand. Carefully, turn it over so that the wax paper is face down on the table. Cut into squares of the same size. To decorate the top try to draw flowers for decoration. If you can cut the cornet with a special edge, it will help in drawing flowers. Note the edge is not an upside down 'V' but looks more like a house with a flat roof.

4. Cut circles in bread using a circle shaped form, butter the bread, and then dip in chives. Poach a quail egg and cut the two ends so that they are flat, and then cut in two. Place the quail egg on top of the bread and then add mayonnaise using a pastry bag. If you have some dried beet it is good to add for color.

Did you know...

Canapé is the French word for couch or sofa. Like a couch is used, the ingredients in a canapé 'sit' on top of the bread, hence the name. Canapés can be made small and served before the main course, or made bigger and served for an outdoor party or picnic.

TIPS AND TRICKS

When you cut bread or sausage, cut lengthwise, not widthwise. While this is more difficult, it minimizes the numbers of pieces you throw away and the number of cuts you have to make. If you buy from a baker or butcher they may be able to cut it this way for you.

*You want all of the canapé to be the same size when you are serving them to guests so they believe they are all equal. *The butter you use on canapé should be softer with more volume, so it's better if you can aerate the butter by beating until smooth and creamy.

CANAPÉ

LETS GET STARTED...

5.   Cut bread with a form shaped any way you like and spread mayonnaise on top. For the first layer add cucumber sliced thin. Next, slice a cucumber half way through one side. Put this piece on the first piece of cucumber by turning one side that you cut back, and the other side forward. Next take ¼ size pieces of cherry tomato, and place one on one side of the canapé and another ingredient that you like on the other. In the photo we have used quail eggs. To finish, take a pastry bag and add a little mayonnaise to help stick these pieces to the form.

6.   Mix cod eggs with one spoon of liquefied gelatin in a bowl. In a second bowl put butter, lemon juice, salt and pepper. First spread the butter mixture on the bread and then add the cod egg mix on top. Do not cut right now, place in the fridge for 20 minutes minimum. Cut pieces later with forms or shapes of your choice. If you prefer, finish with a nice decoration made of butter.

7.   Take bread and spread a good amount of mayonnaise on top. The mayonnaise should be equal to the thickness of the bread. Repeat this step 3 times with 3 different pieces of bread. Then place the layers that have been painted on top of each other with one more piece of bread that has not been touched on top. Put in the fridge for 20 minutes until it has sufficiently hardened, cut into slices and serve.

8.   Use a pastry bag to put a cheese/mayonnaise mixture on top of sliced cucumber. To make it a little more beautiful, add on top a small ingredient with red color, and then a small green leaf to finish.

9.   Spread tomato concasse (see basics) on a piece of bread, and then, using a circle tool, cut out circle shapes in the bread. On top place a rolled anchovy, a mixture of pre-cut vegetables and add a slice of lemon in the middle.

Did you know...

Canapé is a word commonly associated with parties and receptions. Napoleon, the first consul of France, understood that meals could be an enjoyable and fruitful business tool. A great chef accompanied him on many of his trips to provide good meals for the others, improving the overall mood, thereby making it easier to achieve his political goals.

TIPS AND TRICKS

To change the taste a little, use different breads, toast some and not others. This allows you a very easy way to have some variety with minimal effort. Don't forget to mix the colors of the various pieces when you serve for a more beautiful presentation.

*If you make them 1 day before, it will still be ok, but you need to glaze with gelatin so that it will conserve itself. *When you use butter for decoration, you need to be sure that there is no salt inside or it will be very difficult to use.

MINI QUICHE LORRAINE

Mise en place

½ cup (120ml) milk
½ cup (125ml) heavy cream
1 egg, 1 egg yolk
1 lb (450g) Pâte a Pâte without sugar (basics)

Contents
⅓ cup (60g) finely chopped onion
⅛ lb (60g) finely chopped bacon
½ cup (60g) shredded Gruyere cheese
Nutmeg

Recipe Difficulty	Level 1
Prep. Time	15 min
Cook Time	75 min
Servings	30 pieces
Wine	Pouilly-Fuissé or Chardonnay

LETS GET STARTED...

1. Mix together the milk, cream, eggs, egg yolks, salt and pepper. Add nutmeg now if desired. This is called the "appareil".

2. Using a rolling pin, roll a Pâté a Pâté thin (see "basics" for Pâté a Pâté instructions). Ensure to roll extremely thin if you are using very small shapes so that there is space for the food to fit inside.

3. Brush the shapes with butter before putting any dough inside. Push the dough into all the corners leaving a little extra on top for creating a rim around the shape.

4. Fill with bacon, cheese, onion and the appareil prepared earlier. If desired, decorate the rim/edges of the dough on top.

5. Put on a baking sheet and place in the oven preheated to 355 ºF (180 ºC). You can check if it's finished by watching to see when the bottom of the dough is cooked.

*Tip * Use a small bag of dough patted with flour to fill the corners. This is better than fingers because with fingers it's possible to make holes in the dough.*

Did you know...

Quiche is a very popular dish in France, made famous from the region of Lorraine. Lorraine and the neighboring region of Alsace are legendary in France, not just for quiche, but also for the number of times they have changed between French and German control. France used WWI to avenge the annexation by Germany over these two regions.

Quiche Lorraine Crust

TIPS AND TRICKS

A full size quiche lorraine is very good when served with a salad for a light dinner while the mini quiche is very popular to use for a party.

Change the cheese to make quiche roquefort or add smoked salmon for variety.

Quiche Lorraine Oven Prep

LEEK TART

Mise en place

½ cup (120ml) milk
½ cup (125ml) heavy cream
1 egg, 1 egg yolk
1 lbs (450g) Pâté Feuilletée (basics)

Contents
¼ lb (120g) thinly sliced leek
⅛ cup (30ml) heavy

Recipe Difficulty	Level 1
Prep. Time	15 min
Cook Time	75 min
Servings	30 pieces
Wine	Pessac-Léognan
	or Semillon

LETS GET STARTED...

1. Mix together the milk, cream, eggs, egg yolks, salt and pepper. Add nutmeg now if desired. This is called the "appareil".

2. Using a rolling pin roll a Pâté Feuilletée thin. Ensure to roll extremely thin if you are using very small shapes so that there is space for the food to fit inside.

3. Brush the shapes with butter before putting any dough inside. Push the dough into all the corners leaving a little extra on top for creating a rim around the shape. Use a fork to make holes in the dough so it does not rise and ruin the shape.

4. Put the leek in water and boil. Add cream and cook to reduce the volume of liquid.

5. Add with the appareil prepared earlier and place inside the forms you have chosen. If desired, decorate the rim/edges of the dough on top.

6. Put on a baking sheet and place in the oven preheated to 355 ºF (180 ºC). You can check if it's finished by watching to see when the bottom of the dough is cooked.

Tip * Use small bag of dough patted with flour to fill corners. Better than fingers because with fingers it's possible to make holes in the dough.

Did you know...

Flamiche is a recipe made with leek ("poirot" in French). A medal named "Merite agricol" is awarded in France to those who excel in the field of agriculture. The medal is more commonly referred to by its nickname "poirot" because it associated with agriculture and has a green textile, the same color as leek.

Leek Tart Mise en place

TIPS AND TRICKS

If the shape you use for the dish is made of iron, dry it very well after use, otherwise it can rust and your next dish will stick to it. Boil the water first and then add the leek, this way the leek will stay a nice green.

Leek ready for use

MINI PIZZA

Mise en place

1 lb (450g) Pâté Feuilletée (basics)

2 tbsp (20g) finely chopped shallots
Finely chopped garlic for taste
1 sprig thyme & Bay leaf
¾ lb (320g) tomatoes (peeled, seeded & diced)
15 anchovies filets
½ cup (60g) cheese
Olive oil

Recipe Difficulty	Level 1
Prep. Time	15 min
Cook Time	75 min
Servings	30 pieces
Wine	Burgundy Côte-d'Or
	or Pinot Noir

LETS GET STARTED...

1. Using a rolling pin roll a Pâté Feuilletée thin. Ensure to roll extremely thin if you are using very small shapes so that there is space for the food to fit inside.

2. Brush the shapes with butter before putting any dough inside. Push the dough into all corners leaving a little extra on top for creating a rim around the shape. Use a fork to make holes in the dough so it does not rise and ruin the shape.

3. To prepare the tomato concasse, sweat shallots, garlic, thyme, bay leaf with a little olive oil, salt, pepper. Add the tomatoes and cook slowly.

4. Let the tomato concasse cool. When cool, place on top of the dough the tomato concasse first, then the anchovies, olives, cheese, and finish with a drizzle of olive oil.

5. Put on a baking sheet and place in the oven preheated to 355 ºF (180 ºC). You can check if it's finished by watching to see when the bottom of the dough is cooked.

Did you know...

The eminent "Medici" family, who lived in Florence, Italy, has many ties to significant historical events. When Catherine Medici married the French King Henry II in 1533 she took a chef with her to France. It was at this time that the chef started to share Italian cuisine with the court of the French King. This is how food such as pizza or pasta began to make its way throughout France.

Mini Pizza "mise en place"

TIPS AND TRICKS

Using a spatula look under the pasta to make sure the dough is really cooked.

You can also use a more bread-like dough for this appetizer if you like. If you do substitute, cook at the highest temperature you can so that it cooks immediately.

Preparing the forms for the oven

PARMESAN CRISPS

Mise en place

2 cups (225g) grated parmesan cheese
*Dry skin of tomato (for color)
1 sprig thyme

*you can use minced red bell pepper instead

Recipe Difficulty	Level 2
Prep. Time	10 min
Cook Time	40 min
Servings	30 pieces
Wine	Vacqueyras or Syrah

LETS GET STARTED...

1. Blend the shredded or grated parmesan cheese in a blender. Add red bell pepper cut fine (or dry skin of tomato) with thyme and blend again. Ensure that the mixture is blended very fine. You can add herbs if you like in this recipe.

2. Preheat the oven and the baking tray at 355 ºF (180 ºC). To shape these treats, place a baking form (e.g. circle) on top of the baking tray. Make sure to oil the tray so the parmesan crisps won't stick when you try to remove it.

3. Sprinkle the mixture on the baking tray inside of the shape you've chosen (i.e. circle).

4. Make sure a minimum of holes exist between the sprinkles or it will break when you try to remove later from the baking tray. You will notice that the mixture starts to melt on the tray before you put in oven because the tray is hot. This is not a problem.

5. Remove the form you used for the shape, and place the baking tray in the oven at 355 ºF (180 ºC) for 2 to 3 minutes, until the food starts to brown.

6. After brown it is ready to remove. If you remove it from the tray too quickly the piece will break, too slowly and it will not be possible to shape when finished (you can build circles, folds, etc.)

Did you know...

Gruyere is a very popular cheese that comes from the same family as parmesan, from a town called Gruyere in Switzerland. In France, people use a variety called "gruyere parler francais" but despite its widespread use, it is really the wrong name for this cheese as it is actually shredded emmental.

Parmesan Crisps

TIPS AND TRICKS

Heat your baking sheet in the oven before to put the cheese on top. This ensures that the cheese melts immediately and you can keep the shape that you are trying to make. Use fresh parmesan and not pre-cut since pre-cut cheese usually has too much fat removed which is needed for this recipe.

LIGHT TOMATO MOUSSE

Mise en place

¼ lb (100g) tomato (*cucumber, strawberry, etc)
½ leaf (1.25g) of gelatine
Salt and pepper
*substitute or experiment as you like

Recipe Difficulty	Level 2
Prep. Time	10 min
Cook Time	Make 1 day prior
Servings	10 sm. glasses
Wine	Bordeaux or Merlot

LETS GET STARTED...

1. Blend tomato, salt and pepper together. Add garlic, vinegar, and other ingredients you like and blend.   Adjust with garnish for your taste.

2. Pass through a sieve and then add the gelatine. Soften the gelatine first by putting it in water and dissolving a little over heat. If you buy powdered gelatine prepare to the same state.

3. The best way to add gelatine is to first add a little sauce to the gelatine and mix. Then take all the gelatine and mix into the rest of the mousse.

4. Put in refrigerator for minimum 24 hours.

*If you serve cold you need to add a little more salt. Generally add 2 tbsp of salt for 32oz of liquid. If you serve hot use just a little less.

Did you know...

The tomato can also be called the "pomme d'amour". The conquerors imported the tomato to Europe in the 16th century after its discovery in South America. When the tomato came to France it was initially used only for decoration and was not eaten. It was only after the revolution when the French really started to eat the tomato.

Light Tomato Mousse

TIPS AND TRICKS

When you whip the cream, don't make it too thick. If the cream is too thick there will be little white specks in the mousse. If you change the main ingredient from tomato to something drier, add a little more water to compensate.

SOUP

Soup conjures up dueling memories for some people. On one hand you have memories of the soup Mom made, your grandparents, and the good old days. On the other hand, it also reminds some about war or depression, when money was scarce and you could only boil vegetables for a meal. In reality, soup is a dish that despite its nostalgia is not eaten very much as a main course anymore.

This photo shows a decoration found on the bottom of a soup bowl. It represents a time ~1910 when the army's favorite dish was soup.

PARMENTIER

Mise en place

⅔ lb (300g) leek thinly sliced
½ lb (225g) potato cut into triangles
⅓ cup (75ml) heavy cream
1½ cups (350g) water

Recipe Difficulty	Level 1
Prep. Time	15 min
Cook Time	25 min
Servings	5
Wine	Montagny or Chardonnay

1. Place the leek in a small pot and sweat in butter. After 2 or 3 minutes, add water and boil.

2. Add potato, salt and pepper and cook at a slow boil for 20 minutes.

3. Add cream at the end and cook until it achieves a good consistency. If you like you can blend for a different texture but it's not necessary.

Family photo album and who many will think about when they think of soup.

TIPS AND TRICKS

Add the cream at the last minute, and never put the croutons inside the soup before serving. Instead, put them on the table for your guests to add. If you add the croutons too early it absorbs the soup making the dish smaller, and the croutons become soggy. * Cut the potato in a square emincer style to make boiling a little quicker.

GAZPACHO

Mise en place

⅓ lb (150g) bell pepper diced
Bell pepper finely diced for decoration
~1 lb (500g) cucumber diced
~1 lb (500g) tomato (peeled, seeded & diced)
⅓ lb (150g) onion diced
3½ oz (100g) ketchup
Finely chopped garlic, white vinegar, croutons
4¼ fl oz (135 ml) extra virgin olive oil

Recipe Difficulty	Level 1
Prep. Time	15 min
Cook Time	0 min
Servings	8
Wine	Crozes-Hermitage or Syrah

LETS GET STARTED...

Gazpacho is an uncooked soup served cold.

1. Cut bell pepper, cucumber, onion and tomato into pieces to make it easier to blend.

2. Add these vegetables together with garlic, salt, pepper, extra virgin olive oil, vinegar, and then blend. When a good texture is achieved put in the fridge and serve cold.

3. Serve with croutons, for decoration add a fine brunoise (small cubes) of red, yellow, and green bell pepper before to serve.

* Note that when you leave this soup in the fridge the taste seems to grow stronger.

Did you know...

In France, an expression "prendre la cremaillere" means to have a house warming. The tradition is to start a fire in the new house for warmth and cooking, and that is where the "cremallere" will be used. A "cremallere" is a metal tool that has rungs at various lengths to hold the pot/soup over an open fire, so that you can cook at high heat on the bottom rung and then later move the pot to the top rung so that the soup does not burn.

Gazpacho

TIPS AND TRICKS

Serve very cold or with extremely small portions (like Amuse Bouche). Be careful with the spice and make what your guests like, not just what you like.

PAYSANNE SOUP

Mise en place

1 oz (25g) bacon
¼ lb (100g) carrot
¼ lb (100g) zuchini
¼ lb (100g) thinly sliced leek
⅓ lb (150g) potatoes
2½ cups (600g) water

Recipe Difficulty	Level 2
Prep. Time	15 min
Cook Time	25 min
Servings	5
Wine	Chablis white or Chardonnay

LETS GET STARTED...

1. A paysanne soup is a soup with bacon, and vegetables have been cut in paysanne style (see basics). You can change the vegetables as you like.

2. Add bacon to a pot of water and bring to a boil once, then remove from heat.

3. Sweat carrot and zucchini for 2 or 3 minutes, add the bacon, and then add water.

4. Bring to a boil and then add the potatoes. Cook at a slow boil for 20 minutes.

Did you know...

In France the law stipulates that a person can only work 35 hours a week (although exceptions exist). This law and others have evolved the job in the kitchen. For example, in some kitchens the classic technique of cutting triangle shapes for the vegetables in the paysanne soup has changed to cutting cubes, simply because the cubes take a little less time to cut.

Paysanne

TIPS AND TRICKS

The name Paysanne reflects the triangular cut of the vegetables. However, if you find it takes too long to make triangles its ok to use cubes instead.

SOUPE A L'OIGNON

Mise en place

1 lb (500g) thinly sliced onion
2½ cups (650g) water
White wine
1 sprig thyme, Bay Leaf
Chicken stock
Emmental cheese

Recipe Difficulty	Level 2
Prep. Time	15 min
Cook Time	25 min
Servings	5
Wine	Gewurztraminer Alsace if possible

LETS GET STARTED...

1. Melt a generous portion of butter in the pan until it turns a chestnut/beige color. After this color of butter is achieved add the onions and cook. While you cook it is important to get a good color on the onions for flavor.

2. If you want, you can add white wine, thyme, bay leaf, and chicken stock but use a very small amount of thyme or bay leaf because they will overpower the taste of onion and give a taste of tea or wine.

3. Cook slowly and let the color develop. Don't flip or stir the onion too quickly or it will not brown, but also be careful not to let the onions burn on the bottom.

4. Add water after the right color is present, and bring to a boil. Continue to cook at a slow boil.

To make French Onion Soup

1. Place soup in an oven safe soup bowl, top each with croutons (or slice of toasted bread), and sprinkle each with ½ cup (50g) of grated Emmental cheese.

2. Then broil or bake at 450 ºF (230 ºC) until melted and brown. * To make your own croutons cut bread in cubes and roast in a pan with butter and oil (use both both butter and oil because only butter will burn and with just oil there is no taste.

Did you know...

In France, onion soup is said to be the typical dish of a marriage party. It is commonly consumed after weddings in the early morning hours when one has had little or no sleep. Some say it is a great way to start such a difficult day. The onion is a specialty of Lyon, which has been nicknamed the capital of gastronomy in France.

Soupe a L'Oignon

TIPS AND TRICKS

On the top of your soup a'loignon you can add cheese and croutons and roast in the oven to make "Gratinee".

CREAM OF TOMATO

Mise en place

¼ lb (100g) thinly sliced onions
1⅓ lb (600g) tomato (seeded and diced)
3⅓ fl oz (100ml) heavy cream
Rice (handful)
1¼ cups (300ml) water
Tomato concentrate
1 sprig thyme
Bay Leaf

Recipe Difficulty	Level 1
Prep. Time	10 min
Cook Time	25 min
Servings	5
Wine	Beaujolais Red or Pinot Noir

LETS GET STARTED...

1. Start a pan with oil or butter and add onions, tomato, a handful of rice, and cook at a slow boil for 20 minutes minimum.   If you want to use tomato concentrate, thyme, and bay leaf add now.

2. Once cooked, blend, and then add cream until you reach the desired consistency.

3. Note that if you did not remove the tomato skin before cooking you should pass the soup through a sieve before serving.

4. Warm before you serve.

Did you know...

In France there are 4 main families of soup, identified by the name: e.g. Tomato Soup, Tomato Potage, Crème de Tomate and Velouter de Tomate. If you pass soup through a strainer the name becomes 'potage passer', adding cream changes the name to 'crème,' and if you add egg yolk it is then called 'velouter.'

Cream of Tomato

TIPS AND TRICKS

It is better to "monder" the tomatoes before starting as this gives a better taste and texture. If you like a very fine taste, add a little olive oil on top of the soup in a design of your liking.

BISQUE

Mise en place

~1 lb (500g) live rock lobster or shore crabs with shell
3 tbsp tomato concentrate, 2 tbsp olive oil
¼ lb (100g) diced carrot
¼ lb (100g) diced onion
Cognac, Pepper, 1 sprig thyme, Bay Leaf
3⅓ fl oz (100g) white wine
2 tbsp fenouil, 1 tbsp rice, 1 tbsp tarragon
2½ cups (600g) liquid (after cooking)
¼ cup (50g) butter, 6½ tbsp (50g) flour
½ cup (120ml) heavy cream
Cubes of crustacean, 4 tbsp of whisked cream

Recipe Difficulty	Level 3
Prep. Time	20 min
Cook Time	35 min
Servings	4
Wine	Pineau de la Loire or Chenin Blanc

LETS GET STARTED...

1. Heat olive oil in a pan to a very hot temperature. Add crayfish and crabs (any crustace is ok), thyme, bay leaf and cook.

2. Next add carrot and onion and cook until the crustace achieve a good red color. Add tomato concentrate.

3. Break the shells of the crustace in the pan as finely as you can. This helps the flavor of the sauce as it releases the taste of the meat. Add cognac and flambé. Add white wine and boil to remove the alcohol.

4. Add water to approximately ~ ½ inch (1cm) above the ingredients. Add fenouil, rice and cook at a slow boil.

5. Pass through a sift to remove bones, etc.

6. Make a roux of melted butter and flour. Gradually add to the stock (liquid) from above with the cream and cook. When it gets a little thick add tarragon. Blend to make smooth.

7. Put cubes of crustace in the bottom of the bowl and pour the warm bisque over the top. If you like, add 1 soup spoon of whisked crème for decoration and taste.

Did you know...

The name for the base Américaine sauce is an evolution of the sauce "Armoricaine" which comes from the Côtes d'armour region of Bretagne. Bretagne is found in the northwest of France, also known to be the country of the Celtics. It's in this region you can visit the forest of "Broceliande" where Sir Lancelot's famous adventures took place.

Bisque

TIPS AND TRICKS

Make sure to cover the top of the pan with a towel or other material when you break the shells inside. If you don't, your clothes will be covered and very hard to clean! You can use bisque as a very good sauce for any dish that contains crustacean.

EGGS

Most everybody's favorite egg growing up was the chocolate one that many children searched for at Easter. As we grow older and the Easter egg hunt fades into a memory, we recognize the actual symbolism of the egg and its connection with life.

The egg is used as a symbol of life in many religions. The symbolism can be obvious as birds break out of the egg and come to life (as with many other animals). Easter occurs in the spring when you find baby rabbits, chicks, and flowers; overall the new cycle of nature and by analogy the new life. In the calendar of liturgy, Easter is the celebration of the resurrection of Christ, which is also considered the new life for many people.

Orpheus and symbolism

Throughout history, the egg has also been used by many philosophers and systems to explain the creation of the world or as a reflection of new life. An example is the system created by followers Orpheus. Orpheus was a famous Greek poet who legend says could charm animals, coax nature or even stop streams with the beauty of his music and song. His disciples built a theory of the creation of the world around the egg where the egg contained the entire world, good and bad, woman and men, various dualities much like the egg yolk and the egg white, while the shell represents the sky.

SPANISH OMELETTE

Mise en place

12 eggs
¼ lb (120g) diced tomato
¼ cup (40g) thinly sliced onion
¼ cup (40g) thinly sliced red bell pepper
¼ cup (40g) thinly sliced green bell pepper
Finely chopped garlic for taste
1 tbsp butter
*Vegetable mix you like as an option.

Recipe Difficulty	Level 1
Prep. Time	10 min
Cook Time	15 min
Servings	4
Wine	Pouilly Fumé or Sauvignon Blanc

1. This omelette is distinguished by having a shape that is flat. Inside it can contain any number of various ingredients that are mixed. Above you will see a traditional recipe.

2. Heat a fry pan with olive oil, add bell pepper and cook for 2 minutes. After the first minute add onion and garlic.

3. Next add the cubes of tomato and cook over low heat for 10 minutes. Mix all ingredients with eggs in a bowl, and then cook in a fry pan with butter.

4. When you make your omelette, if you are able to keep it flat you can call it 'omelette plat espagnol.' The taste (vegetables for example) you include in the recipe does not change the name of the dish like it normally would for other dishes.

Spanish Omelette

TIPS AND TRICKS

Use your imagination for the garnish of this dish. This recipe is great as it can be made quickly when you are pressed for time.

FRENCH OMELETTE

Mise en place

12 Eggs

Recipe Difficulty	Level 1
Prep. Time	5 min
Cook Time	3 min. per
Servings	4 omelettes
Wine	Champagne or Dry Sparkling

LETS GET STARTED...

1. Warm a fry pan with a little butter. Melt the butter but don't let it change color.

2. In a bowl mix the eggs very well and then put in the fry pan. Move/mix the eggs a little while they start to cook so they don't burn or color.

3. At one point (eggs are still a little runny) stop moving the pan, and try to keep the majority of the runny part on one side of the fry pan.

4. Start to close the omelette by turning the finished side over one side at a time. Use as many steps as needed, but ideally it takes 2 turns from each side to get finished.

5. When you have folded the eggs completely into an omelette shape it is ready to put on a plate.

*One technique is to hold a plate upside down on top of the frying pan, and turn the pan upside down with the plate. There is a better chance of not breaking the omelette this way.

Did you know...

If you want to work in a French restaurant, you better know how to cook an omelette! It is commonly known that for the interview the chef may ask you to make a French omelette and this is your only chance to succeed. If you don't make this omelette the right way, he tells you to take your knives and go home, because to the chef it means that you don't know how to cook anything.

Flip Technique

TIPS AND TRICKS

If you put some drops of vinegar on top of the omelette it will help with digestion.

When you are ready to place the omelette on the plate, your palm needs to be under the pan handle to flip it on the plate easily.

French Omelette

SCRAMBLED EGGS

Mise en place

12 eggs
2 tbsp (30g) butter
5 tbsp chives
*heavy cream

Recipe Difficulty	Level 1
Prep. Time	10 min
Cook Time	8 min
Servings	4
Wine	Sancerre white or Sauvignon Blanc

LETS GET STARTED...

1. The "right way" to make scrambled eggs means this is not a broken omelette. You need to see both white and yellow parts of the egg when finished to be successful.

2. Put an oven safe bowl on top (inside but not touching the water) of another pot that has slowly boiling water, this method of cooking is called using a "Bain Marie" (you can also use a double boiler).

3. Melt butter in the bowl, and just slightly break the eggs with a fork before adding. This is done so that they will cook a little differently.

4. Cook the eggs very slowly (not too hot over the heat) and you will see the eggs start to change color.

5. When the color has started to appear mix the eggs completely. Mix in chives or whatever other ingredients you might like.

6. Add a small amount of cream when it is ready to serve.

To Make A Fun Decoration with Eggs

Separate the white and egg yolk from an egg. Take egg yolks and pass through a sieve (to remove the skin around the egg yolk). Heat a fry pan warm enough to cook the egg yolk, but not change the color. Take the egg yolk and using a spoon or a cornet draw a design in the pan. When the egg yolk has cooked a little, add the egg whites. Add the egg whites very close to the pan and a little to the side so that the force from the pour doesn't ruin your design. The white will cook over top of the yolk. Add ingredients inside if you like and fold over the white sides to close.

Did you know...

If you measure the weight of an egg you may be amazed at how consistently the measurements are 30g for the egg white, 20g for the egg yolk, and 12g for the shell. The average hen use to lay approximately 100 eggs each year, however selective breeding has some averages over 250 per year now.

Beautiful 'egg' coat

TIPS AND TRICKS

If you want to win this recipe every time, cook in a bain marie. This ensures the eggs cannot burn.

EGG RECIPES

Mise en place

Eggs
Bread
Butter

Recipe Difficulty	Level 1
Prep. Time	see below
Cook Time	see below
Servings	various
Wine	Champagne or Dry Sparkling

'Boiled Eggs In The Shell'

1. Boil water and cook eggs for 3 ¼ to 3 ½ min. The white will be cooked but the yolk remains soft.

2. These eggs taste good with "mouillette" (bread fingers) toasted in butter on a skillet. Use the bread fingers to dip in the egg yolk.   It's easier if you use an egg cutter than a knife to cut off the top of the egg.

'Soft Boiled Eggs'

1. Boil water and cook eggs for 5 min. The egg white is cooked, and the egg yolk is soft, but it should be easy to remove the shell. Use a spoon and break the entire shell of the egg very well.

2. Once you have broken all of the shell you can peel with your hand. Be careful because the egg yolk is still soft. *If it is hard to remove the shell then it's possible you did not get under the first skin.

'Hard Boiled Eggs'

1. Boil water and cook eggs for 9 min.

Eggs with "mouillette"

TIPS AND TRICKS

For soft boiled eggs use the freshest that you can find for the best taste. In France, 'extra fresh' eggs are by law, within 11 days of being laid. When you cook eggs, add an onion peel and it will change the color of the shell.

SHELLFISH

Shellfish is a very popular type of food eaten frequently throughout the world. Popular examples include crabs, lobsters, clams, mussels and oysters. While "fish" is in the name shellfish are not actually considered a fish despite their association with water. Shellfish are considered to have wonderful things inside, just like the treasure box depicted here. We hope you find some treasure in this chapters' recipes.

Pirate's treasure

One viewpoint on world creation, on the 2nd day you can see water split in two, one part for sky, other part for the ground.

Water and evolution share a storied past with each other from religion to evolutionary theories put forth by Darwin. Some evolutionists hypothesize that humans evolved from sea species that crawled out from the sea, became simple land creatures that through adaptation of the years eventually became what we are today. Some religious accounts state that God created water on day 5 and added sea creatures to live there. Christians commonly refer to fish throughout their history and several of the disciples were referred to as fishermen The Ichthys is the symbol taken by Christians that resembles a fish and in Greek actually is the word for fish.

Regardless of your beliefs you will see that the kingdom of the sea figures prominently in history and is found throughout many traditions in the world.

ESCARGOT SALAD

Mise en place

48 snails (raw)
3 oz (80g) diced ham
¼ lb (120g) tomato concasse (see basics)
*1 ladle chicken stock (preferred)
2 tbsp thinly sliced shallots
Garlic, Bay leaf
Salad greens and Vinaigrette

Recipe Difficulty	Level 1
Prep. Time	15 min
Cook Time	20 min
Servings	4
Wine	Burgundy Côte-d"Or or Pinot Noir

LETS GET STARTED...

1. Pre-preparation To prepare to cook snails, put them in a pan with cold water and bring very slowly to a boil. This causes the snails to leave their shells and they will ultimately be cooked before they go back inside. *Be careful because you need to heat the pan slowly for this to happen. Most people buy snails from a store already prepared.

2. Heat olive oil in a fry pan. Add snails, salt and pepper and sauté.

3. Add cubes of ham and continue to cook. Don't move the pan too much so that the ingredients do have a chance to cook. Remove some of the fat in the pan if you find there is too much.

4. Add tomato concasse, chicken stock (if available), shallots, bay leaf, garlic, and continue to cook.

5. Prepare a salad with vinaigrette and serve with the snails.

Did you know...

In France there are 3 big families of shellfish that live on the ground. The most famous and largest of these is the escargot de Bourgogne. If you are very lucky and find a snail where the shell coil is sinistral (left handed), keep it because nearly all the snails are dextral.

Escargot Salad

TIPS AND TRICKS

If you want to use fresh snails, remember that you need to keep them in the dark for 15 days before use. This is because the snails eat vegetables and herbs that can make a person sick. The 15 days allow adequate time for the snails' systems to be clean and therefore ready to eat.

Escargot "Parmentier"

Mise en place

48 snails (pieces)
4 large potatoes (old)
Big Salts
7/8 Cups leek (emincer)
Thyme
Bay leaf

Recipe Difficulty	Level 1
Prep. Time	10 min
Cook Time	30 min
Servings	4
Wine	Burgundy (white) or Chardonnay

Lets Get Started...

1. Pre-preparation - To prepare to cook snails, put them in a pan with cold water and bring very slowly to a boil. This causes the snails to leave their shells and they will ultimately be cooked before they go back inside. *Be careful because you need to heat the pan slowly for this to happen. Most people buy snails from a store already prepared.

2. Heat butter in a fry pan, add thyme & bay leaf (optional). Add snails, salt and pepper and cook.

POTATO MASH

1. Take a potato and put on wax paper with coarse salt (like a bed) on a baking tray. Cook in an oven preheated to 320 °F (160 °C). When you can place a knife inside the potato and remove cleanly it is ready. Cut the potato in half and scoop the majority of the potato out from the inside of the skin with a spoon. Put the potato shell back in the oven as you will use this later for presentation (see picture.)

2. Boil the leek in water for 5/6 minutes. Mix the leek together with the mashed potato in a bowl. Put the mixture on a plate as bed for serving the potato skins and snails. If you can use a circle form to keep a shape it helps with presentation.

3. Take the potato shells from the oven and brush with butter (or oil) so they shine.

4. Put potato shells on top of mush and put the snails inside.

Did you know...

How to tell the difference between a male and a female snail? If you don't know how it's ok as most are hermaphrodites. A hermaphrodite is an organism that possesses both male and female genitalia.

Escargot Parmentier

TIPS AND TRICKS

To make a more beautiful presentation of this dish, brush the shell of the potato with butter so it is shining. For variety, you can use the same recipe with whelk "bulot" snails.

MOULES MARINIERE

Mise en place

4½ lbs (1600g) mussels (incl. shell)
1¼ cup (200g) finely chopped shallots
¾ cup (200ml) white wine
1 sprig thyme
½ bay leaf

Recipe Difficulty	Level 1
Prep. Time	15 min
Cook Time	10 min
Servings	4 (as main dish)
Wine	Pouilly Fumé or Sauvignon Blanc

LETS GET STARTED...

1. Pre-preparation: Clean the mussels and put them in cold water. Next, if the shell of the mussel is closed it is still alive; if the shell is open it is dead. Never use a dead mussel because it may cause food poisoning. To remove the "beard", place the mussel flat in your hand and grab the beard. Pull the beard from the smaller/front part of the shell towards the larger part of the shell to remove.

2. Melt butter in a pan and add shallots. Add 1 sprig thyme, ½ bay leaf, and a little pepper. Add the mussels, white wine and cook. Cover with a lid or plate to keep the steam/flavor inside the pot.

3. The mussels are cooked when their shells open. As soon as the mussel has opened remove them from the pot otherwise the mussel will overcook and become hard.

4. The liquid that is left after you have finished cooking the mussels is considered a stock. You can use this liquid for other recipes or sauces.

Did you know...

Mussels find starfish to be one of their predators and require a host fish to be able to complete the reproductive process.

Moules Mariniere

TIPS AND TRICKS

Ensure that you wash the mussels very well before you start or there will be little grains of dirt inside your dish. While cooking, remove the mussel as soon as it has opened. If you cook it longer the mussel will become dry and hard.

Mussels Sauce Poulette

Mise en place

4½ lbs (1600g) mussels (incl. shell)
1¼ cups (200g) finely chopped shallots
¾ cup (200ml) white wine
1 sprig thyme
½ bay leaf

½ cup (60g) Flour
¼ cup (60g) Butter
1 cup (245ml) heavy cream
Changes depending on quantity of juice after cooking see
recipe for details

Recipe Difficulty	Level 2
Prep. Time	15 min
Cook Time	10 min
Servings	4 (as main dish)
Wine	Pouilly Fumé or Sauvignon Blanc

Lets Get Started...

1. Pre-preparation: Use the same steps listed in Moules Mariniere for the mussels.

2. Dissolve butter in pan and add shallots, thyme, ½ bay leaf and a little pepper. Add the mussels, white wine and cook. Cover with a lid or plate to keep the steam/flavor inside the pot.

3. The mussels are cooked when their shells open. As soon as the mussel has opened remove them from the pot otherwise the mussel will overcook and become hard. The liquid that is left after cooking is considered a stock that you can use for other recipes or sauces, including sauce poulette.

4. Remove half the shell off the mussels and using a knife loosen the mussel from the bottom shell that is left. The purpose for doing this is to make it easier to eat when the meal is served.

To make the poulette sauce:

5. Prepare 3¼ cup (750ml) juice from the mussels (after cooking), ½ cup (60g) of flour and ¼ cup (60g) of butter and 1 cup (245ml) of cream. You can change the amount of cream and juice in the recipe; however the total needs to remain at ~ 1 quart (1 Litre). If you have less than 1quart (1 Litre) of juice, scale down the butter and flour by an equivalent ratio.

6. Melt the butter first and then mix in the flour (flour needs a minimum of 3 minutes to cook). Ensure you watch the time to pass the 3 minute mark. Add the mussels' juice and cream to this base, and then use a hand mixer to blend. Pour the sauce over the mussels. Don't be shy because the mussels need the taste. Add garnish on top as you like to make more beautiful.

Did you know...

The technique to cultivate mussels is a relatively new invention found by chance in the 13th century. A boat from Ireland had shipwrecked stranding the crew off the coast of France. When they strung up nets to catch fish, they found mussels growing on the wooden poles flourished, and thus created a popular mussel farming technique still used today.

Mussels Sauce Poulette

TIPS AND TRICKS

Bouchot (smaller) mussels are preferred over the larger mussels from Spain or the Mediterranean sea for this recipe. Cook with a dry white wine, not sweet.

FRIED MUSSELS WITH TARTAR

Mise en place

Mussels, White wine, Flour, Eggs, Breadcrumbs, Toothpicks
1 cup (250ml) vegetable oil, 1 egg yolk, 1 tbsp mustard
1 egg
3 tbsp (30g) finely chopped shallots
1½ tbsp (30g) finely chopped capers
1½ tbsp (30g) finely chopped pickles
1½ tbsp finely chopped Chives
1 tsp Dijon mustard

Recipe Difficulty	Level 1
Prep. Time	10 min
Cook Time	15 min
Servings	4
Wine	Pineau de la Loire or Chenin Blanc

LETS GET STARTED...

1. Pre-preparation: Use the same steps listed in Moules Mariniere for the mussels.

2. Add mussels in a pan with white wine and cook. Cover with a lid or plate to keep the flavour inside the pot. When the mussel has opened it is cooked. As soon as the mussel has opened remove it, because otherwise it will overcook and become hard. Remove the mussels from the shells.

3. Prepare 3 plates; one with flour, another with eggs, and a third with breadcrumbs. Place the mussel in flour, pat to remove any excess flour, then place in the eggs, and then in the breadcrumbs. Ensure the entire mussel gets covered at each step. Skewer on toothpicks.

4. Preheat a pot with oil to 355 ºF (180ºC). Place the skewered mussels inside.

*If you like keep one shell for decoration on the plate so they know what it is.

Tartar Sauce

1. Prepare a mayonnaise by mixing the egg yolk with mustard and a little salt. Whisk all ingredients in a bowl with the vegetable oil. Add shallots, capers, pickles, chives and one hard boiled egg into this mayonnaise, add salt and pepper for taste. As an option add dijon mustard to your taste. If the sauce is too thin, add more oil and whisk quickly.

Did you know...

France has a shape similar to a hexagon where 3 of the six sides touch the sea. It's only in these sea-bordering regions where mussels have been eaten for a long time. In all the other parts of France, it was impossible for the food to spread throughout the country until the discovery of the train car and refrigeration. Imagine in your part of the country how your diet would be different without these inventions.

Fried Mussels Sauce Tartare

TIPS AND TRICKS

If you want to keep the mussels crispy, don't cover the top of the pan, because the steam will stay in the pan and make the bread soggy.

Huitre Glacee (Oysters)

Mise en place

48 oysters
Béarnaise Sauce
White vinegar
2 tbsp finely chopped shallots
Crushed black pepper
2 tbsp finely chopped tarragon
2 egg yolks
⅔ cup (150g) butter
5 fl oz (150ml) heavy cream
Coarse Salt

Recipe Difficulty	Level 3
Prep. Time	25 min
Cook Time	15 min
Servings	4
Wine	Champagne or Dry Sparkling

Lets Get Started...

1.   Open oysters following the instructions in the Oyster preparation section.

2.   To make the béarnaise sauce, add just enough white vinegar to cover the bottom of a sauce pan. Sweat shallots, crushed black pepper, and tarragon together in the pan and when 90% of vinegar is gone, remove from heat. Let the pan sit as the sauce needs to cool to approx. 185 ºF (85ºC) before adding egg yolks. When the pan has cooled add a ½ egg shell of water with the egg yolks and mix very quickly to create an emulsion. Return to low heat mixing constantly ensuring that you touch every part of the pan, otherwise the eggs will cook and become an omelet. If the pan is getting too hot (>200 ºF or 95ºC) remove from the heat for a few seconds continuing to mix and put back on the heat after. The sauce should start to thicken after approximately 3 min.

3.   Once desired consistency is achieved, remove from heat. Add melted butter, small amounts at a time, to the side of the pan and mix in a circle motion. The sauce should start to look like a mayonnaise. Add salt and pepper (salt only if necessary), and a little leftover tarragon for color. Never put the sauce back on the heat directly or it will break. A little easier method is to use a bain marie (see glossary.)

4.   Whip cream in a separate bowl. Then in a new bowl, whisk equal parts of whipped cream and sauce. Check for taste, add pepper if you like, and add oyster juice to the mix if there is some remaining in the oysters. Be careful if you add salt because oyster juice can be very salty.

5.   To serve place coarse salt in a hollow circular mold on top of a plate and sprinkle water over top so that the salt doesn't move. Put the oyster flat on the salt.

6.   Cover the oyster completely with sauce otherwise it will dry when it is cooked. Put in the oven on broil and remove when brown coloration is achieved.

Did you know...

It has been said that one piece of sand can stop an enterprise. At the same time, that same grain of sand turns into one beautiful pearl within an oyster. How? A pearl starts as a grain of sand that enters the oyster. The oyster protects itself by enveloping the grain of sand, thereby creating a pearl.

Huitre Glacee (Oysters)

TIPS AND TRICKS

Before you add the sauce, loosen the oyster from the shell so that it is easier to eat after it is cooked.

SCALLOPS ST. JACQUES

Mise en place

4 sea scallops
4 scallop shells
4 tbsp of white wine
Coarse Salt
2 tbsp thinly sliced chives
Lemon to your taste
¼ cup (50g) butter
Food coloring

Recipe Difficulty	Level 1
Prep. Time	10 min
Cook Time	10 min
Servings	4
Wine	Burgundy (white) or Chardonnay

LETS GET STARTED...

1. Brush butter in the scallop shells, add salt and pepper. Add 1 scallop (salt and pepper the scallop also) with white wine inside the shell.

2. Put on a bed of coarse salt in a frying pan and place all in an oven at 375 °F (190 °C) for ~10 minutes depending on your oven. Using a bed of salt keeps the scallop shell flat so the liquid remains inside. Use this liquid after cooking to make sauce.

3. Take the liquid from inside the shell and cook in a pan. If there is a lot of juice cook to reduce.

4. When you have a good flavor, add butter and a taste of lemon and swirl to get a consistent sauce. When ready, add chives and pour the sauce over the scallops in the shell and serve.

*Use coarse salt for decoration. An option is to mix in bowl with a little color (e.g. blue) and then add white salt at end for nice mix and use for the plate.

** Number of servings are based upon presentation, increase portions if desired.

Did you know...

The smallest member of the scallops family commercially available is called the calico, the largest being the sea scallop. The shell is sometimes used as a basis for the 'benitier' in a church as the shell is large enough to use to hold the holy water.

Scallops St. Jacques

TIPS AND TRICKS

This dish is better if you make it for a minimum of 4 people because you need to have enough liquid to make your sauce. If you only make this for 1 or 2 people add a little cream to have enough sauce.

SCALLOPS BROCHETTE

Mise en place

24 scallops
24 pieces of cubed bell pepper
Flour, Olive oil, 8 brochette sticks
2 tbsp finely chopped shallots
4 tbsp white wine
2 tbsp heavy cream
Lemon for taste
¼ cup (50g) butter

Recipe Difficulty	Level 1
Prep. Time	15 min
Cook Time	10 min
Servings	4
Wine	Alsace Riesling or Dry Riesling

LETS GET STARTED...

1. Cube bell peppers (green and red) the same size as the scallops if possible. Alternate the scallops and peppers on a kebab/brochette. If the scallops have been frozen add a little flour before cooking.

2. Cook in butter or olive oil (pan should be hot but not too hot). Baste in the juice from the pan and do not turn.

3. The scallops cook quickly, even 5 minutes may be too much so be careful. It depends on the temperature you use and the size of the scallops.

4. For the sauce, sweat shallots, white wine, salt and pepper and cook to reduce the volume of liquid. Add cream and perform a reduction.

5. Finish by adding some lemon, a little butter and swirling in the pan to achieve a good consistency for the sauce.

Did you know...

In southwest of Europe, you can find many signs of people who support the fable of St. Jacques, also known as St. James the Great. In fact, many people called 'Jacquaire' make a pilgrimage in this area following St. Jacque's route. You can identify these people because they wear a bag or a shell from a scallop during the venture.

Scallops Brochette

TIPS AND TRICKS

Always ensure there is enough hot butter or fat in the pan when you start to cook the scallops. If you don't, the water from the scallops will leak out into the pan and boil, causing your scallops to be of sub-par taste with no coloration.

CRAB & LOBSTER "PARMENTIER"

Mise en place

Court Bouillon (see 'basics')
½ cup (100g) white butter (see 'basics')
¼ lb (120g) baking potatoes
2 eggs
⅔ cup (160ml) milk
⅔ cup (80g) flour
¼ lb (100g) crab meat
12 rock lobster medallions

Recipe Difficulty	Level 2
Prep. Time	10 min
Cook Time	40 min
Servings	4
Wine	Meursault or Buttery Chardonnay

LETS GET STARTED...

1. Peel and then boil baking potatoes, remove when they are ready. When you can insert a knife and remove cleanly the potatoes are ready.

2. Mash and place in a bowl and then using a whisk add egg, then milk, then flour, then salt and pepper.

3. Prepare a court bouillon large enough to poach the crab in. Weigh the crab, for every 2.2lbs (1kg) it needs 20 minutes to cook, adjust as necessary.

4. Once the crab has cooked, remove the meat from the shells, cut in small pieces and place in a bowl.

5. Add potatoes and mix with a spatula. Then make into a mini pancake shape and fry.

6. Put the rock lobster in the same court bouillon and poach. Follow the instructions above for cooking time. After cooking, take the rock lobster and cut down each side to remove the middle shell. Remove the meat and cut into medallion pieces.

7. Serve the crab 'pancake' with rock lobster medallions on top. Put coarse salt and pepper on top and then cover with white butter. *Note you can change rock lobster and use a shrimp, rock shrimp (langoustine) or another shellfish that you like.

Did you know...

In the world of potatoes there is one exception, the blue potato. The 'vitalote' has a black skin and a violet color on the inside. If you use these potatoes you will find the taste to be the same as other potatoes, but your guests will see something they have never seen before.

Crab & Lobster "Parmentier"

TIPS AND TRICKS

Use this recipe for cocktail parties and if you have no crab, change with any other crustacean. Use old potatoes because they are better to use in a mush. Mix together with the other ingredients while hot.

PANEQUET DE CRAB

Mise en place

Court Bouillon (see 'basics')
4 sheets of brique pastry (or phyllo)
Herbs
Zucchini, red bell pepper, etc
8 crab claws (meat only) or ~7oz (200g)
Vegetables of your choice (diced)

Recipe Difficulty	Level 2
Prep. Time	15 min
Cook Time	30 min
Servings	4
Wine	Burgundy (Red) or Pinot Noir

LETS GET STARTED...

1. Prepare a court bouillon large enough to poach the crab in. Weigh the crab, for every 2.2lbs (1kg) it needs 20 minutes to cook, adjust as necessary. Poach the crab and then remove.

2. Next, take a sheet of brique and cut a slice large enough so you can cover the herbs in the middle when finished. Brush one leaf with butter and place herbs on top in an attractive pattern.

3. Cover or close with another piece of brique and then place the crab, vegetables, and salt and pepper inside. Don't add too much inside because you have to fold into a cube or packet shape.

4. Fold closed and place in an oven preheated to 340 ºF (170 ºC) and cook. You need the oven to be hot or there is a chance the packet will break.

*One option is to add to the presentation of brique, skin of zucchini, red bell pepper, etc. as long as you cook them first (and they are very finely cut.)

Did you know...

The name 'panequet' is used for this recipe because of the shape of the dish and the dough. The pretty name "panequet" means 'small bread' and is a combination of two words, the Italian word 'pane' which means bread, and the French word paquet, which means a small package. Loosely translated 'a small package of crab' is what you will be delivering to your guests.

Panequet de Crab

TIPS AND TRICKS

Start to cook your panequet with the side folded shut face down so that it sticks together. If the leaves are facing upwards, it will open when it cooks, and you will lose your shape.

Opening The Oyster

Tips and Tricks

You need to be careful if you try to open your own oysters as the shells can be sharp and the technique can be difficult for some. Only you can judge if you should attempt this and can complete safely.

Preparation:
Wear gloves or with a cloth in your left hand, take the oyster and position it on top of the cloth with the smallest side closest to your left hand and the largest side facing up and close to the right hand. With your right hand put your right thumb on the blade near the tip so that if the blade goes through your finger stops the blade from going too far.

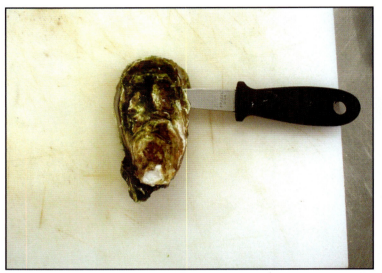

Where to insert the oyster tool

Oysters should be imagined as having 3 equal parts. About ⅓ away from large end is the entrance to the mouth. The entrance to the mouth is the area where you want to insert the oyster tool. See picture on the next page. When you insert the tool, use a little force, and pivot right to left to pry open. Once opened, you will not need to use as much force. Pry open further and point the sharp end of the tool upwards towards the shell, and run the knife around the length of the shell to separate and cut away the muscle. If you do it properly the shell removes easily leaving the oyster inside.

Oyster appearance after opening

Dip the oyster in cold water using a wavy motion so that all the dirt is removed from under the layers and set the oyster aside on a plate.

LOBSTER

"In ancient civilizations, one would turn to the stars to answer life's questions"

The sky would 'speak' to the people about life and the seasons. There was a special star and sign created which is called "Cancer" today. Using the stars for guidance was extremely popular and spread through all societies from the Greek to the Romans to the Europeans. This is where the zodiac signs you find in your morning newspaper come from. One of the oldest signs showing the lobster and its use in ancient society can be found in "Planisphere" in the temple of "Denderah" located in Egypt. The astronomical ceiling showed the different zodiac constellations that people followed at the time. While the sign of "Cancer" is associated with the crab you will see many times the picture does not resemble a crab at all, often with a lobster drawn in its place. Throughout time the sign of Cancer has changed even being associated with the lobster at one point. In the most famous fable, the crab won its spot in the sky when it was rewarded for trying to help the monster Hydra in its fight against Hercules.

When the stars turn in the sky it means that time is passing, which also means the seasons are changing. For a chef, the best season to use lobster is May to September when the quality is at its best. When lobster is out of season, it is of course more expensive and thus used just for special occasions.

Ancient calendar with stars drawn on the outside ring

Lobster In Court Bouillon

Mise en place

Court bouillon (see 'basics')
⅔ cup (150ml) white butter (see 'basics')
2 Lobsters of ~1 lb (500g) each

Recipe Difficulty	Level 1
Prep. Time	15 min
Cook Time	20 min
Servings	4
Wine	Meursault or Buttery Chardonnay

Lets Get Started...

1. Prepare a court bouillon large enough to put in the lobster and poach. Weigh the lobster, for every 2.2lbs (1kg) it needs 20 minutes to cook. Adjust as necessary, for example cook for 9 minutes if the lobster is 1lb (450g). Do not add the weight of the lobsters together when you do this calculation as the cook time and calculation is per lobster.

2. Take the poached lobster and cut along sides of the shell at the tail to remove the middle section. Cut but don't break the claws so you can use for decoration. Use fingers to loosen and remove meat. Cut the main part of the lobster and put back in serving plate.

3. Add garnish on top and brush with butter for shine.

Prepare white butter sauce

4. Sweat shallots with white vinegar and pepper. Cook until almost all the vinegar is gone.

5. Add white wine and again cook until almost all liquid is gone. *If you add any spice add with the white wine.

6. Add a little cream and boil to make the sauce thicker. Add cold butter (in cubes) and swirl. Use a crustacean butter if you have one.

7. As an option, add herbs to the sauce, mix and serve.

Did you know...

'Homard' or the lobster, is considered the royal animal of the sea and as such is called the "Plat du Roi" or "dish of Kings". "Plat du Roi" is now a popular expression in France that somebody would say to the chef to indicate a dish was fantastic. A second name for the lobster is "Cardinal de Mer". The lobster gets this name because it achieves a red coat when it is cooked, just like the coat of a Cardinal.

Lobster in Court Bouillon

TIPS AND TRICKS

Live lobsters will give you the best results because once a lobster is dead, the meat changes to a texture more like cotton. For variety, substitute a béarnaise sauce for the white butter sauce as it goes very well with this recipe. See instructions in the Huitre Glacee recipe.

GRILLED LOBSTER

Mise en place

2 lobsters of ~1 lb (450g) each
Olive oil
Lemon
Chives

Recipe Difficulty	Level 2
Prep. Time	10 min
Cook Time	10 min
Servings	4
Wine	Pouilly-Fuissé or Chardonnay

LETS GET STARTED...

1. Cut the lobster in the middle of the two shells near the head. Push down hard on the handle to go all the way through the lobster and then cut towards the middle of the head. Turn the knife towards the tail and slice the length of the body to finish. Clean the lobster and remove the liver and coral.

2. Put salt, pepper, and a little olive oil (or regular oil) on top of the meat while it is still in the shell.

3. Prepare a grill to a very hot temperature and then put the lobster down meat first, keeping it in one section of the grill if you can. Turn once 45º to make nice decoration lines.

4. Turn over and cook the remainder of the time with the shell side touching the grill to keep the liquid inside.

5. Later crack the claw and put in the oven at 355 ºF (180 ºC.)

6. Serve after with juice of lemon and chives.

 * Always remove the smaller sizes of meat first because they cook quicker than the claw. ** If you prefer, cook the claw in the oven over fennel stalks for a good aroma.

Did you know...

While most people believe the lobster has 8 or 12 legs, the lobster actually has 10. Interestingly the lobster is capable of regenerating appendages when needed but be sure to check you picked the right animal while you have them cooking on the grill!

Grilled Lobster

TIPS AND TRICKS

Start with a very hot grill and sear the lobster meat very quickly, then turn and cook the remainder with the shell side on the grill. This keeps the juice in the shell with the meat for a better taste.

LOBSTER AMERICAINE

Mise en place

1¼ cup (300ml) bisque using lobster
2 lobsters of ~1 lb (450g) each
2 tbsp finely chopped shallots
1 tbsp diced carrot
2 tbsp olive oil
Garlic
1 tbsp finely chopped tarragon
¼ lb (100g) tomatoes diced

Recipe Difficulty	Level 3
Prep. Time	10 min
Cook Time	15 min
Servings	4
Wine	Condrieu (white) or Viognier

LETS GET STARTED...

1. Push down hard on the handle to go all the way through the lobster and then cut towards the middle of the head. Turn the knife towards the tail and slice the length of the body to finish. Clean the lobster and remove the liver and coral.

2. Make or warm the bisque in one pan (see 'soups') but use lobster instead of rock lobster or crabs if possible.

3. In a second pan, sear the lobster in olive oil. Reduce the heat and sweat shallots, carrot, garlic, tarragon, tomatoes, salt and pepper in the pan.

4. Remove the meat when it is ready, the shell should have turned red. Add a ladle of bisque through a strainer to the pan and simmer, blend the sauce to finish.

5. Remove the meat from the shells, put back in with the sauce and serve. Keep the shells and include for presentation if you like.

Did you know...

Some lobster but not all have a 'corail' (which in English means coral). If you find the corail it will be green in color, but it changes to red after being cooked.

Lobster Americaine

TIPS AND TRICKS

For all the recipes using sauce, if you find the corail when you cut the lobster, pass it through a strainer, and add to the sauce when you are finishing for a liason. Be careful not to let the sauce boil again or it will be ruined.

LOBSTER THERMIDOR

Mise en place

Court bouillon (see 'basics')
2 lobsters ~1lb (450g) each
4 tbsp béarnaise sauce
White vinegar, 2 tbsp finely chopped shallots
Crushed black pepper
2 tbsp finely chopped tarragon
3 egg yolks
⅔ cup (150ml) melted butter
4 tbsp heavy cream
1 tsp Dijon mustard
Breadcrumbs

Recipe Difficulty	Level 2
Prep. Time	20 min
Cook Time	30 min
Servings	4
Wine	Condrieu (white) or Viognier

LETS GET STARTED...

1. Prepare a court bouillon large enough to put in the lobster and poach. Weigh the lobster, for every 2.2lbs (1kg) it needs 20 minutes to cook. Adjust as necessary, for example cook for 9 minutes if the lobster is 1lb (450g). Do not add the weight of the lobsters together when you do this calculation as the cook time and calculation is per lobster.

2. When cooled, push down hard on the handle to go all the way through the lobster and then cut towards the middle of the head. Turn the knife towards the tail and slice the length of the body to finish. Leave the half shells intact as you will use for presentation and serving. Put these on a baking sheet for later.

3. To make the béarnaise sauce, add just enough white vinegar to cover the bottom of a sauce pan. Place shallots, black pepper, and tarragon together in the pan, and when 90% of vinegar is gone, remove from heat. Let the pan sit, as the sauce needs to cool (to approx. 185 °F / 85 °C) before adding egg yolks. When the pan has cooled add ½ an egg shell of water with the egg yolks and mix. Mix constantly ensuring that you touch every part of the pan, otherwise the eggs will cook and become an omelet. If the pan is getting too hot (200 °F / 95 °C) remove from heat for a few seconds, continuing to mix, and put back on heat after. The sauce should start to thicken after ~3 minutes.

4. Once desired consistency is achieved, remove from the heat. Start to add liquid butter, small amounts at a time, to the side of the pan and mix in a circle motion. The sauce should start to look like a mayonnaise. Add salt and pepper (salt only if necessary), and a little leftover tarragon for color. Never put the sauce back on the heat directly or it will break. A little easier method is to use a bain marie (see basics.)

5. Preheat the broiler. Mix together two spoons of whipped cream, béarnaise, and bread crumbs. Add dijon mustard for taste. Pour on top of the meat (still in the shell) and broil in the oven until golden brown. Make sure you cover all of the lobster meat with sauce but not on the shell because the shell will burn.

Did you know...

During the French revolution in 1792, the people changed the names of all the months. The old July and August became "Thermidor" which meant the month of the Roman bath or "Therm". On February 18th 1799, Napoleon Bonaparte ended the revolution and became the emperor. In the year 1806, Napoleon put the 'old' calendar (the one used today) back into effect. See the illustrations on the following page.

Lobster Thermidor

TIPS AND TRICKS

Using the best quality lobster will make your dish taste the best. Usually these lobsters come from the sea, in France that is from the region of Bretagne.

"THERMIDOR"

Napoleon was responsible for many things during his tenure, the metric system (1801) being one of those credited to him. The calendar (below) was also his initiative in 1806. If you look closely you will see the "old" (vieux style) calendar includes months such as Novemeber and December, the "new" calendar months named Fruitidor and Thermidor.

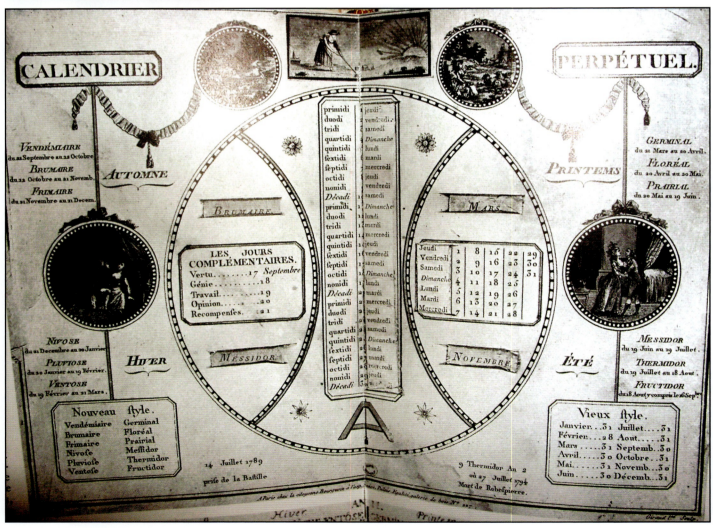

FISH

Fish is an extremely popular dish served around the world, the most famous market being the Tsujiki fish market in Tokyo, Japan. Tsujiki transacts over 400 different species of fish weighing over 2 million tons annually. This far exceeds the 150 tons of fish that flow through the largest wholesale food market in the world, Rungis which is located in Paris, France. While tuna is most associated with the Tsujiki market, salmon and mussels are what flow most through Paris. You will find some very good tasting dishes for both salmon and mussels in the following chapter.

Recently at Tsujiki market a blue fin tuna sold for $92/lb.

Suprisingly, that is not a record, as on Jan. 1st 2001, one sold for ~$175k USD or $400/lb.

Tsujiki Market, Japan

BREADED TROUT FILET

Mise en place

4 trout of ~½ lb (250g) each
24 medium sized potatoes (tourner)
4 lemons for garnish
2 eggs
1 tbsp vegetable oil
Salt, Pepper & Breadcrumbs
See recipe for details

Recipe Difficulty	Level 2
Prep. Time	20 min
Cook Time	25 min
Servings	4
Wine	Alsace Riesling
	or Dry Riesling

LETS GET STARTED...

1. Ready the trout filets and 3 pans; one for an eggs/oil combination, one for bread-crumbs, and one for flour.

2. First put fish in the flour and cover completely (including the top). Next place the filet in the egg mix, cover completely, then flip and cover the other side also. Put in the breadcrumb mix, fillet part down to finish. Sift breadcrumbs over the top (other side) of the fish. Place carefully on the cutting board and using the dull side of a knife push imprints into fish to give criss-cross like appearance. When finished try to keep head the right way up so it looks like a fish.

3. Heat oil in a pan and put the filet part of fish in first (the fish is basically upside down with the meat side down on the pan). To turn over, put a spatula under the head and down the length of the fish, put hands on battered part for balance, then carefully pick up and turn. Use a spoon and baste with the liquid in the pan.

4. Take potatoes and prepare using the tourner technique. Boil in water until you can insert a knife and remove cleanly. Finish by roasting in the fry pan with butter for a few minutes to make crispy.

 * If you have kept the head, don't grab the trout by the head or eyeballs as some people would like these parts to remain covered with the breadcrumbs.

Did you know...

Trout and salmon come from the same family, the salmonidae. You can see that they are in the same family because they only have one fin, and this is the only family that you can recognize this way. In case you were wondering, the fin has fat inside.

Breaded Trout Filet

TIPS AND TRICKS

Put the filet side in the pan first and when it is time to turn your fish, place your spatula lengthwise under the head towards the tail. You can touch the top of the fish with your hand (because it is not hot) in order to keep the fish in one piece. This way its ready to go on the plate without additional turns.

SEARED SALMON FILET

Mise en place

1⅓ lbs (600g) salmon in 4 portions
2½ tbsp mustard seed
½ cup (120ml) olive oil
2 lemons
Red bell pepper diced

Recipe Difficulty	Level 1
Prep. Time	10 min
Cook Time	15 min
Servings	4
Wine	Burgundy (Red) or Pinot Noir

LETS GET STARTED...

1. Take a salmon filet and cut a nice design in the skin on the back (see picture for an example). The filet should be approximately 2 inches wide.

2. Add salt and pepper on both sides and put in a very hot pan with the skin side of the salmon down.

3. After initially searing the meat, turn down the heat and let it cook. As it cooks you will see the color change on the way. The top of the filet should still be a little pink when it is finished. Be careful not to overcook the fish.

4. Make a sauce by mixing mustard seed, olive oil, lemon, and red bell pepper together.

Did you know...

Civilization has advanced in several ways changing the way we eat. The import/export business evolved substantially in the 19th century allowing numerous different products to move between countries where it wasn't possible before. The bourgeoisie and nobility also created novel tools to use with the different foods that you eat (e.g. a knife used 'sole' ly for eating fish.)

Seared Salmon Filet

TIPS AND TRICKS

Start to cook on the skin side and never turn the fish. To make a beautiful plate, decorate with salmon eggs, but ensure you do not cook them.

GRAVLAX (SALMON)

Mise en place

~2 lbs (1kg) Salmon
⅓ lb (160g) Coarse Salt
½ cup (90g) Sugar
1 cup (50g) Dill, chopped
½ tbsp (5g) Pepper

Recipe Difficulty	Level 1
Prep. Time	1 day prior
Cook Time	10 min
Servings	8 (appetizer size)
Wine	Burgundy (white) or Chardonnay

LETS GET STARTED...

1. Mix together coarse salt, sugar, dill, and pepper. Lay the salmon filet in a bed of the mixture.

2. Then cover the top of the salmon with the same mixture and place in the fridge for 6 or 7 hours. * Note that if you keep in the mixture too long then the salmon gets hard and salty.

3. Wash everything off the salmon (remove from mixture.)

4. While holding the salmon over a pan, sprinkle some dill and olive oil over top. Turn the salmon so that the meat is in the oil bed (with the dill) and you can marinade in the fridge for a longer time if you like.

5. To serve to guests slice very, very thin. You should always be able to see the knife while it is cutting inside the salmon.

Did you know...

In the old calendar, April 1st was actually the first day of the year in some countries, and as such it was thought to be a very happy day. When the calendar changed in the 17th century, many did not recognize the new date and those were sent on fools errands. Tradition now says we should play a funny joke on our friends on April 1st. In France, the traditional joke was to put a fish on the back of another person.

GravLax (Salmon)

TIPS AND TRICKS

Eat with roasted bread. Be careful not to leave the salmon in the mixture too long, as it will become dry, hard, and have a salty taste.

SALMON TARTARE WITH CAPE

Mise en place

½ lb (225g) chopped salmon
½ lb (225g) smoked salmon (thin filets)
5 tsp finely chopped chives
5 tsp olive oil
5 tsp thinly sliced shallots
Lemon juice for taste

Recipe Difficulty	Level 1
Prep. Time	20 min
Cook Time	0 min
Servings	4
Wine	Alsace Pinot Gris or Pinot Gris

LETS GET STARTED...

1. If you need to remove the skin, take your filet of salmon, and using a knife, cut through a small piece near the tail to find the skin. When removing the skin, do not move the knife along the fish, but pull the skin over the knife. Move your hand with knife back and forth to achieve a cutting motion, but leave the knife in the same place on board. This works best with a knife that is not too sharp so that you can apply a bit of force but not cut through the skin.

2. Note that the brown part of salmon is ok to eat but appearance is poor, so it's up to you if you use it. Don't cut the cubes of salmon too thin because the lemon will dry and shrink when added to the salmon.

3. Cut the salmon and add together in a bowl with lemon juice, very thin chives, olive oil, salt and pepper, and shallots.

4. Place plastic wrap in a different round bowl and cover the plastic with thin slices of smoked salmon.

5. Put the first salmon mix on top and then gather the plastic wrap together into a firm ball. Remove air by putting holes in plastic and put in the fridge before serving.

Note that Tartare de sous cape de saumon fume is the actual name for this recipe.

Did you know...

This recipe name translated means salmon under cape, and references a part of normal dress used throughout the 17th century. The cape was a fine piece of material that protected the person wrapped inside, as the smoked salmon cape does for the tartare. The most popular people known today that wore a cape are the Three Musketeers. That book was written by Alexandre Dumas, whose body has gone to the Pantheon in 2002. Likely Mr. Dumas never expected to be included in a recipe book.

Salmon Tartare with Cape

TIPS AND TRICKS

This dish tastes much better if kept in the fridge for 1 hour before you serve. If you can, serve with little pieces of bread that have been toasted.

SALMON MOUSSE

Mise en place

2¼ lbs (1kg) salmon cubed
32 fl oz. (1 Litre) heavy cream
4 (120g) egg whites
1 tbsp salt
~½ tbsp pepper

Recipe Difficulty	Level 1
Prep. Time	
Cook Time	use as needed for
Servings	other recipes
Wine	Condrieu (white)
	or Viognier

LETS GET STARTED...

1. Put salmon in a cold blender and add salt and pepper. Mix only until the salmon is broken and then let the mixture sit as the blender has to stay cool and the salt needs time to work with the collagen of the fish.

2. Add egg whites and blend. When mixed, let the mixture rest again so the salmon and the blender cool down.

3. Add cream and slowly mix. Stop just before it is mixed completely (there should be very little cream left when you finish) and then finish mixing by hand.

*If you are using a very fresh fish, add a little less egg white because too much egg white will make the mousse hard. **Be careful when adding salt as the amount needs to match the amount of meat being used.

Did you know...

The dark pieces on the salmon come from the parts that touch the skin of the fish. These pieces are less attractive, so people assume they are not good, but they are fine to eat. Just be careful when you use them as these dark pieces change the color and appearance of your dish.

Salmon Mousse 'Mise en Place'

Salmon Mousse

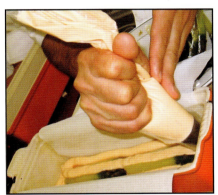

Salmon Mousse in use

TIPS AND TRICKS

White eggs change the texture of the mousse. If you want a thick mousse, add more eggs. For a softer texture, remove some.

BRANDADE (COD)

Mise en place

1 lb cod (480g)
⅓ cup (80ml) milk
Water to poach
1 sprig thyme & 1 bay leaf
½ lb (240g) peeled baking potato
4 tbsp olive oil
Pepper & Herbs

Recipe Difficulty	Level 2
Prep. Time	15 min
Cook Time	30 min
Servings	4
Wine	Burgundy (white) or Chardonnay

LETS GET STARTED...

1. Poach the cod filet in milk with water, thyme, bay leaf, and pepper. Do not add salt because the fish is typically already very salty.

2. Prepare a potato mash by putting unpeeled potato in water and boiling. After it is cooked peel and mash. Remember the potato is ready when you can insert a knife and then remove cleanly.

3. Poach the cod slowly and when you see foam on the top, remove the pot from the heat as it will cook itself. When you touch the filet and the meat can separate it is ready.

4. Put the cod in a blender with the potato mush and olive oil. Add salt and pepper for taste, or other herbs and spices as you like.

Did you know...

Brandade is a specialty of the south of France, but it is actually a fish of the cold sea. This dry, salty fish is caught by fishermen who travel a very long way and eventually return with the catch. This recipe is typical of food that did not always exist in France, but was integrated because of its use in other cultures.

Brandade (Cod)

TIPS AND TRICKS

For best results, put your salt water cod in cold water for 24 hours before you use to remove the salts. If not, your recipe could be very salty.

STUFFED TURBOT

Mise en place

2½ lbs (1.2kg) turbot (whole)
¾ lb (320g) mushroom mix diced
4 tbsp finely chopped shallots
2 tbsp finely chopped parsley
2 tbsp finely chopped chives
Court bouillon with no vinegar (see basics)
Sauce:
2 cups (460ml) court bouillon
3 tbsp (40g) butter
⅓ cup (40g) flour
½ cup (115ml) heavy cream

Recipe Difficulty	Level 3
Prep. Time	50 min
Cook Time	30 min
Servings	4
Wine	Burgundy Red or Pinot Noir

LETS GET STARTED...

1. Sprinkle salt and pepper over the fish and put on top of plastic wrap with the white part on film.

2. Cook the mushrooms in a little butter, but not too quickly. Add salt and pepper, and if there is a lot of liquid perform a reduction.

3. Sweat shallots. Add parsley and chives. Take the mix and put together inside the fish and then wrap with plastic wrap.

4. Secure the fish loosely to a board and then put in a court bouillon to poach. Ideally use 175 °F (80 °C) for a temperature because if it is much warmer the fish will move and ruin the shape.

5. When finished remove the skin (black and white) with a knife. The skin comes away relatively easy. Remove the last part of the bones (on the outer limits of the sides.)

6. Take butter and dissolve in a pan over medium heat. When dissolved add flour, cook for 1 minute, then add liquid from court bouillon where you poached the fish (use a whisk to mix.)

7. Add cream and cook for 4 to 5 minutes and blend to finish. Pour on top of the fish for serving. You can use any other fish sauce that you like with this recipe.

*To stuff the fish use a salmon mousse or duxelle (see glossary) instead if you like.

Did you know...

Turbot is a fish with bi-colored skin, white on bottom and black on top. This fish swims horizontally all the time and nature provided a two-colored coat so that the fish that pass by over top see not the fish but the black stone of the ocean while the fish that pass under see only the white from the light above.

Stuffed Turbot

TIPS AND TRICKS

This fish gets cold very quickly, so if you want to have the better taste, eat as soon as it is ready. Warm your plate in the oven before serving to help keep warm.

Stuffed Whiting

Mise en place

2 lbs (1kg) whiting (4 pieces)
⅓ lb (160g) julienne leek
⅓ lb (160g) julienne carrot
1⅓ lb (600g) mousse of salmon
Vegetables for decoration
⅔ cup (150g) white butter (see 'basics')

Recipe Difficulty	Level 3
Prep. Time	60 min
Cook Time	15 min
Servings	4
Wine	Pouilly-Fuissé or Chardonnay

Lets Get Started...

1. Boil and remove the julienne of leek and carrot. Add salt, pepper and butter.

2. Take the filet (with bones removed) and stuff with a julienne of vegetables. Ensure to keep a flat shape when you do this and leave a rim around the fish clean.

3. Next, using a pastry bag, cover the entire fish and vegetables with a salmon (or other type) mousse. Use a spatula and smooth the mousse on top but be sure the vegetables remain completely covered.

4. Once finished, you can decorate the top of the mousse with a red pepper skin heart or zucchini flowers and carrot, etc. as long as they have been previously cooked.

5. Steam the fish at 210 ºF (100 ºC) for roughly 8 minutes. If you don't have a steamer prepare one pot with boiling water, and then place the whiting inside on top of another dish like a shelf so that it does not touch the water. Close the lid and let the fish cook in the steam.

6. After it is ready, put on a towel to blot out some of the water. Serve with white butter on top or on the side.

Did you know...

In France "merlan surnaime" is the name of a person who cuts hair. This name was given to hairdressers because in the time of the king, the fashion for the man was to wear a white wig on his head that was the same silver and white color of the merlan (whiting.)

Stuffed Whiting

TIPS AND TRICKS

If you want to have a beautiful dish, don't add too much julienne of vegetables because it is hard to cover attractively with salmon mousse on the outside.

CRAZED WHITING

Mise en place

2 lbs (1kg) whiting (4 pieces)
4 olives
4 toothpicks
Flour
Oil

Recipe Difficulty	Level 1
Prep. Time	30 min
Cook Time	20 min
Servings	4
Wine	Alsace Riesling or Dry Riesling

1. Cover the whiting in flour. Put the tail in the fish mouth with an olive and use a toothpick to close.

2. Heat oil and put fish inside when the temperature is 355 °F (180 °C). Cook for 4-5 minutes.

3. Remove and blot on paper towel. Take out the toothpick and serve with lemon and turned potatoes.

Crazed Whiting

Did you know...

The actual name of this dish in French is "merlan en colère" which means "whiting in anger."

When you fry a whiting (merlan) the eyes of the fish turn white and hazy, which led to an expression in France used for a man in love. When you gaze into the eyes of your significant other and have that hazy lost in love look, it is called the eyes of fried merlan.

TIPS AND TRICKS

This is a dangerous recipe because you cook with oil. To help ensure you don't burn yourself, use a very deep pot and cover with a grill after you put the fish in helping to keep the oil inside.

CHICKEN

The French are very sentimental about the chicken as the two have shared a very long history together starting back in the time of the Romans. The Romans call the country where the Celtic live the "Gaule" and the man who lives there the "Gaulois". In Latin, "Gallus" means "Chicken". Like the "Gaulois", the chicken is considered to be a very proud and brave animal. It is for these traits that the French took the chicken to be a symbol of France. The French take the "Brave" part of the animal and use this trait for symbolism in war, and the "French Pride" is well known throughout the world today.

The chicken is always the first to wake in the morning, look at the sunlight, and say to the world 'be careful' or 'vigilant' with its call. Perhaps telling us it is time to stand up and do something productive. In Asian culture you will see on the top of cultural buildings a symbol of each year of their zodiac calendar which includes the dog, monkey, chicken, pig etc. If you look closely you will notice on these buildings the chicken will always be the first symbol facing east as it was always the animal to predict the rise of the sun. The monkey will be in the west as it was always considered a night animal.

One joke often used to temper the French pride is to point out that the chicken is admittedly always on top and very proud, but always also has one foot in manure.

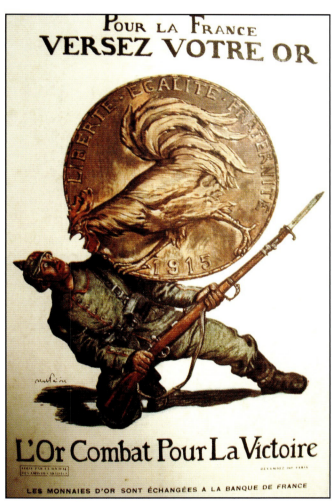

Poster found during the war

ROAST CHICKEN

Mise en place

1 chicken of 2½ lbs (1.2kg)
16 small potatoes (30g each) (tourner)
1 onion (peel and cut in quarters)
Bay Leaf, 1 sprig thyme, Garlic, Butter
Sauce, Water
⅛ lb (50g) cubed carrot
⅛ lb (50g) cubed onion
3.5 fl. oz (100ml) white wine

Recipe Difficulty	Level 1
Prep. Time	20 min
Cook Time	80 min
Servings	4
Wine	Alsace Pinot Gris or Pinot Gris

LETS GET STARTED...

1. Prepare chicken as outlined in the basics section. Remember to put salt, pepper, bay leaf & thyme (optional) inside the chicken before closing.

Roasting:

2. Preheat the oven to 390 ºF (200 ºC). Put the chicken in a baking tray and cover with quite a bit of butter, salt and pepper. Try to place butter in places where it will stay on top of the chicken. Add garlic, bay leaf, thyme, potatoes and onion to the tray. Use a tray that fits your chicken very well so that there is only a little space and will help keep the butter from burning.

3. Put legs to one side and cook for 20 minutes in the oven. Flip to the other side and cook for another 20 minutes and then finish cooking for 20 minutes with the legs up.

4. When the chicken is finished, the juice is clear when it comes out; if it is still bloody then it is not done. Baste each time you flip with the liquid from the pan.

Sauce:

1. When the chicken has finished roasting, remove the chicken and potatoes and place to the side.

2. Take the dish and now add carrot, onion and cook on the stove. Add a good amount of white wine to the pan and use a brush to remove anything that has stuck to the bottom or sides. It is this 'stuck' part that has good flavour for the sauce. Add water to cover the vegetables, and cook at a slow boil for 15 minutes.

3. Watch the sauce for you may need to add more water or increase the amount of cooking time to achieve a good taste and consistency of the sauce. The color should be brown/dark brown. Pass the sauce through a sieve and serve with the chicken and potatoes.

Did you know...

The dish presentation you see in the picture is the classical form named gondola, just like the boat you can find in Venice, Italy. The napkin is folded into a shape so that it looks just like a gondola. The inside of the napkin is filled with aluminum foil so that it is strong enough to keep its form.

Roast Chicken

TIPS AND TRICKS

Try not to break the skin of the chicken when you turn it in the pan. Use a turning stick below the legs or in the hole at the rear. When your chicken has finished roasting add a little salt and pepper on top before you eat for a better taste.

"MINUTE" MUSHROOM CHICKEN

Mise en place

1⅓ lbs (600g) chicken
4 tbsp finely chopped shallots
~1 lb (480g) sliced Paris mushrooms
3.5 fl. oz (100ml) white wine
4 tbsp butter
Chives for decoration

Recipe Difficulty	Level 1
Prep. Time	15 min
Cook Time	15 min
Servings	4
Wine	Pessac-Léognan White or Semillon

LETS GET STARTED...

1. Slice the chicken very fine and brush an oven safe plate with butter.

2. Sprinkle salt on the plate, add chicken and then place in the oven at 355 ºF (180 ºC) The chicken is very thin so it cooks very quickly (<5 minutes.). When the plate is hot it should be ready.

3. Add butter to a fry pan and heat. Add mushrooms and flip after they have some color (approx. 1 min). Add shallots and cook.

4. Add white wine and cook to reduce the volume of liquid to approximately ½. The white wine adds taste but make sure to cook long enough to remove the alcohol.

5. Add more butter and then move pan very quickly in circular motion Add salt and pepper. Put the mushrooms and sauce over the chicken.

6. Sprinkle chives on top of the dish for presentation.

Did you know...

This recipe is called "Minute du Poulet" in French because it literally takes only minutes to cook! This is a great recipe for when you are entertaining friends because you can get everything ready before they arrive and only spend minutes in the kitchen cooking!

Chicken & Mushrooms

TIPS AND TRICKS

Use an oven safe plate and when you see the chicken is white, remove it from the oven. This will happen very quickly because the chicken is cut very thin.

CHICKEN FRICASSEE

Mise en place

4 legs of chicken
½ lb (225g) julienne carrot
½ lb (225g) julienne leek
⅓ lb (135g) thinly sliced shallot
1 sprig thyme & 1 bay leaf
⅜ lb (170g) tomato (peeled, seeded & diced)
½ lb (225g) thinly sliced mushrooms
Garlic & Chicken stock

Recipe Difficulty	Level 1
Prep. Time	20 min
Cook Time	30 min
Servings	4
Wine	Languedoc Red or Zinfandel

LETS GET STARTED...

1. Fricasse is a term that essentially means: water, sauce, and cook a long time.

2. Heat a pan with butter. When a hazelnut/beige color is achieved, put salt and pepper on the chicken and roast for color.

3. Add the carrot, leek, shallots and mushrooms and sweat. The vegetables should cook very quickly.

4. Add tomatoes, thyme, bay leaf, salt and pepper with chicken stock (if you have). Add chicken and cook until nice brown color is achieved. Now leave on very low heat and cover with aluminum foil. Cooking this way lets the flavour come out.

5. Remove the chicken, slice, and put on a plate.

6. Take the juice and vegetables from the pot and place on top of the chicken.

Did you know...

You can find many different qualities of chicken. Two main types of chickens are farmer and industrial bred. The largest difference in the quality is that the farmer chickens usually have more space to roam and experience the sunlight. The industrial chickens usually have a more tender texture because they don't get to use their muscles as often.

Chicken Fricassee

TIPS AND TRICKS

If you use farmer bred chickens you will find a more authentic taste. However, if you use industrial bred chickens you may save a few dollars. This will depend on your specific situation and market.

CHICKEN CURRY

Mise en place

1½ lbs (700g) sliced chicken strips
¾ cup (120g) thinly sliced shallots
⅔ cup (160g) heavy cream
Curry powder for personal taste
Chicken stock

Recipe Difficulty	Level 1
Prep. Time	15 min
Cook Time	10 min
Servings	4
Wine	Alsace Gewurztraminer
	or Gewurztraminer

LETS GET STARTED...

1. Put oil in pan and heat. When you see the first smoke in the pan it is ready to use.

2. Put salt and pepper on the chicken and place in the pan. Flip when the color starts to change.

3. After the chicken is done add shallots and sprinkle on the curry for taste. Add chicken stock if you have and cream and bring to boil. When bubbles look thick and big, it is ready.

4. Add salt and pepper again for taste.

Did you know...

In France the 'Poulet Bresse' is the best quality chicken available. The Bresse chicken has red hair, white body, and blue feet which are co-incidentally the same colors as the flag of France - red, white, and blue.

Chicken Curry

TIPS AND TRICKS

This recipe will taste best when it is made at the last minute. Use a curry that most importantly suits your taste; spicy or moderate flavor will work well.

Chicken "En Voile"

Mise en place

1½ lbs (650g) chicken (thin filets)
½ cup (100g) shredded emmental cheese
1 (50g) large egg
¾ cup (175ml) milk
⅜ cup (50g) flour
1 tsp oil
Tomato concasse (see basics)

Recipe Difficulty	Level 1
Prep. Time	15 min
Cook Time	15 min
Servings	4
Wine	Burgundy Red or Pinot Noir

Lets Get Started...

1. Whisk cheese, egg, salt and pepper together in a bowl. Add just enough milk to cover the ingredients and then add a little flour to make the liquid thicker. As soon as it looks thick, stop (not too thick or thin). It should look a little lumpy with a similar consistency to pancake dough.

2. Put oil in a pan and heat. When you see the first smoke from the pan it is ready to use.

3. Add salt and pepper on the chicken, dip in the dough, and put in the pan. When there is some color on one side flip and cook the other side.

4. Put the chicken on a paper towel when it is done to remove some of the grease, and then put on the plate.

5. Serve with a sauce that is like a tomato concasse.

Did you know...

This is a great recipe to use for young children because the crepe, cheese, and chicken are very easy to make and almost always a hit with kids. Maybe it's your favorite too!

Chicken "en Voile"

TIPS AND TRICKS

If you are going to put this dish in the oven to warm it up before you serve, brush the dish with butter so that the food will not stick to the plate.

Chicken "Au Vinaigre"

Mise en place

4 legs of chicken
4 tbsp finely chopped shallots
½ tsp garlic & 1½ tbsp tarragon
½ lb (200g) tomato (peeled, seeded & diced)
1 sprig thyme 1 bay leaf
5 tbsp red wine vinegar
1½ tbsp tarragon
3 ladles of water (chicken stock preferred)
Vegetables for garnish
Roux - 1 tbsp oil & 1 tbsp flour

Recipe Difficulty	Level 1
Prep. Time	15 min
Cook Time	45 min
Servings	4
Wine	Bordeaux Fronsac or Merlot

Lets Get Started...

1. Heat a pan with butter inside. When the butter is a chestnut/beige color it is ready to use.

2. Add salt and pepper on the chicken and put in the frying pan. When the chicken is finished remove from the pan so it doesn't continue to cook.

3. Cook shallots, garlic, tomato, thyme and bay leaf. When it is ready add red wine vinegar, tarragon and boil to remove some of the acid from the vinegar. Add Chicken stock if you have some.

4. Put vegetables, stock, etc. together now with chicken and cook with aluminum on top to keep steam and flavour inside.

5. Put in oven for 40 minutes and cook at 320 °F (160 °C.)

6. Take the liquid from the pan above and pour through a strainer. If the sauce needs to be thicker, mix the oil and flour in a separate bowl. Take a small amount of this mixture and add to the sauce.

7. Put chicken in the sauce and baste completely. Serve with pearl onions, glazed or the vegetable of your choice.

Did you know...

In France, in the time of King Henry IV (who died in 1610), the people had very little to no money, and therefore could not afford to eat meat. King Henry IV recognized people needed to eat some amount of meat and decreed that every Sunday the people would eat chicken with a recipe called "Poule au pot"... note "Poule" is female chicken or "hen."

Chicken "Au Vinaigre"

TIPS AND TRICKS

This recipe is already very tasty because of the vegetables added so you do not need to use your best vinegar; normal red wine vinegar will be adequate. For a better dish, put one soup spoon of fresh chopped tarragon in the sauce when it is finished cooking.

DUCK A L'ORANGE

Mise en place

2 pieces magret duck breast
8 tbsp red vinegar
3 tbsp sugar
4 oranges
Zest of orange
Stock of chicken

Recipe Difficulty	Level 2
Prep. Time	10 min
Cook Time	20 min
Servings	4
Wine	Burgundy Red or Pinot Noir

LETS GET STARTED...

1. Use fingers to 'square' the duck and remove the excess skin and fat. Remove the nerve on top where the blood goes in (if there is one.)

2. Put the duck in a hot pan with the skin/fat side down, and get a good color. If there is too much fat in the pan remove some. Flip the duck to roast and get a good color on the other side.

3. When you get that good color flip again so the fat is on the bottom, remove from the fire, and let cook slowly in a warm oven at approximately 250 °F (120 °C) for 10 minutes (leave the oven door open). It is important to remove the meat from the fire so it doesn't overcook.

Orange Sauce

1. Put red vinegar and sugar (vinegar in first) in a pan and dissolve to make a caramel type sauce. When caramel sauce is ready add juice from the oranges and boil.

2. Add chicken stock (if available), cook but do not reduce too much or the sauce will be too sweet. To finish and make the sauce a little richer, add a spoon of butter and swirl in the pan. If the sauce appears to have too much liquid, slowly add a mixture of oil and flour until you reach the desired consistency.

3. When the duck is ready, slice thin and put in sauce a l'orange and then serve.

*If you want to make your sauce better, add zest of orange, but first put the rind in cold water and boil to remove the bitter taste from the skin.

Did you know...

Magret de canard does not refer to a regular duck, but for one that has been raised with an endless supply of food. Magret de canard is very tender whereas a normal duck has a drier texture. In France you can eat the magret de canard when the meat is pink because of its tenderness. If you use a normal filet of duck and call it magret de canard it is actually considered a very serious offence and you can go to jail.

Duck a l'orange

TIPS AND TRICKS

It is better to cook your magret and then keep it warm in the oven. This is so the meat can rest, giving time for the juice to spread and not stay in the middle. For sauce l'orange, it is much better to squeeze fresh oranges than use juice from a bottle or can.

CHARTREUSE OF DUCK

Mise en place

tool: 4 circle forms of ~3 inches (8 cm) diameter
Wax paper
Carrot & Turnip
1 egg
Potatoes
Leek or cabbage (preferred)
Duck Liver (cubed) optional
Foie gras (sliced)
1 cup (225ml) heavy cream

Recipe Difficulty	Level 3+
Prep. Time	(This is difficult and
Cook Time	time consuming)
Servings	
Wine	Alsace
	Gewurztraminer or
	Gewurztraminer

LETS GET STARTED...

1. **Decoration** for the outside rim: Choose vegetables with different colors like carrot and turnip. Cut jardinière style and cook glacer (see basics). Choose a circle shape and cut wax paper the length of the inside circle. Place the circle on top of a piece of wax paper, and after buttering the inside of circle form place there the wax paper cut earlier. Place vegetables around the circle in an alternating pattern.

2. **Cooking**: Boil the leek and potatoes (remove skin first) and then mash. Prepare a hot pan and cook the foie gras first to get a good color. Since the foie gras has a lot of fat there is no need to add butter. As the foie gras cooks baste with a spoon frequently. When the foie gras has a beautiful color, take out of the pan and put to the side to finish cooking slowly. Add duck liver to the pan and cook with shallots, leek and potato (adding salt & pepper for taste). Add back the foie gras fat and put the meat back in the pan.

3. **Stuffing** / "Farce" : We now want to add a stuffing in the middle of this circle, examples could be a mash of potatoes or leek. Add the duck liver, in the blender with salt for ~1 minute, 1 egg white and blend. Add pepper and 1cup (225ml) of cream and blend slowly. Spread against the vegetable decoration and place the filling of your choice in the middle of the circle and push in a little to help give the form of a cake.

4. **Finishing**: Fry a small filet of foie gras, place on top and pour a little sauce from the pan around the top to finish. Add one or two big pieces of pepper or coarse salt for appearance.

Did you know...

Usually the sounds we make for the duck are "Quack, quack" but in France they say "coin coin". There is one duck, the canard de barbarie which is a family of duck that has no voice. This duck says "_____".

Chartreuse of Duck

TIPS AND TRICKS

It is not possible to make this dish without a circle form. It is difficult to finish, but the end result is beautiful. It is important to place the vegetables in the form at the same angle after cooking as when initially measured. Remove the circle at the very last minute or the vegetables will dry.

DUCK MARINATED IN RED WINE

Mise en place

4 legs of duck
⅓ lb (160g) diced onion
⅓ lb (160g) diced carrot
1 sprig thyme
1 bay leaf
3⅓ cups (800ml) red wine

Recipe Difficulty	Level 1
Prep. Time	15 min
Cook Time	12 hours
Servings	4
Wine	Languedoc Red or Zinfandel

LETS GET STARTED...

1. Clean the duck of any excess fat, nerves, etc. that you may find.

2. Add salt and pepper to the duck, and put in a hot fry pan. Ensure to get good color.

3. In a fry pan cook onion and carrot with thyme and bay leaf. Flip ingredients as necessary. Add red wine and boil.

4. Mix all ingredients together and cook in a normal oven at 160 ºF (70 ºC) for 12 hours. Cover the pot to make sure the water does not escape.

5. Serve when it is ready and do not let it sit.

Did you know...

This recipe comes from the traditional food that was eaten in France a long time ago. People hunted duck frequently in the wild and it was soon discovered that a marinade was needed to make the meat tender.

Civet de Canard (Duck) Marine

TIPS AND TRICKS

Use a strong (yet inexpensive) red wine; 14 percent for example. Dry the duck from the red wine before you roast otherwise the liquid will boil and change how the duck cooks.

SLOW ROASTED DUCK

Mise en place

4 leg of duck
⅔ cup (200g) coarse salt
1 bay leaf
1 sprig thyme
2¼ lbs (1kg) of duck fat

Recipe Difficulty	Level 2
Prep. Time	1 day before
Cook Time	120 min.
Servings	4
Wine	Beaujolais Red or Pinot Noir

1. Take a leg of duck and remove the majority of the fat that you find. Rub the meat with coarse salt. Add bay leaf, thyme, some pepper (but not too much) and leave for 24 hours.

2. Melt a pot of fat and keep between minimum 165 °F (75 °C) and 185 °F (85 °C) maximum. Add the meat and cook for 2 hours minimum. You need to ensure that the temperature stays within the range specified.

Slow Roasted Duck

Did you know...

In France, the best region to find duck is in the southwest near Toulose or Sarlat. To make this recipe well, you need to use a duck that is very tender and has lots of fat (like for magret de canard) as the extra fat helps make it tender and juicy.

TIPS AND TRICKS

Buy a box of duck fat to use with this recipe because there may not be enough in the duck itself. It is better if you cook the day before and eat the day after. Warm the duck slowly before serving.

BEEF

One fable talks about the bull Minotaur. This animal is considered to be a representation of all the bad things you can find in someone's heart. The bull Minotaur is commonly portrayed in the middle of a labyrinth, symbolic as the heart is in the middle of the body.

Thésée tue le Minotaure. Vase grec.
Ve siècle avant J.-C.

Legend tells of a Mr. Theseus who went to the labyrinth and killed the bull Minotaur and then used the string of Arian (the string of the sky and the ground), to find his way back outside again. The symbolism is that to clear your heart or mind of bad thoughts or evils you must kill your bull Minotaur, and then commonly use a 'string' or a friend's help to get out again and back to normal life after such a significant change.

BEEF WELLINGTON

Mise en place

1¾ lbs (800g) beef filet
½ lb (250g) diced mushrooms
3 tbsp finely chopped shallots
1½ fl. oz (40ml) heavy cream
2 - 8.5 x 11 inch sheets of puff pastry
Egg yolk (for brushing)
Crepe
1 (60g) eggs
¾ cups (200ml) milk
½ cup (60g) flour
1 tsp oil

Recipe Difficulty	Level 3
Prep. Time	30 min
Cook Time	60 min
Servings	4
Wine	Bordeaux or
	Cabernet Sauvignon

LETS GET STARTED...

1. Melt oil and butter in hot pan, add mushrooms and cook. Next add shallots, salt and pepper but don't move the pan around too much or temperature will drop and the mushrooms will boil. Brown the mushrooms and once ready, add white wine and cook to reduce the volume of liquid. Next add cream and emulsify.

2. Put the filet of beef in a hot fry pan and roast. Get good color on all sides, but don't cook the meat all the way through because that will take place later in the oven.

3. Brush a rectangle of puff pasty with egg yolk and place a crepe cut down to the same size over top. Place the beef on top of the crepe and press the mushroom mix onto the filet of beef and cover completely (~¼ inch/6 mm thickness). Finish the inside by covering the meat with another crepe placed over top. *Crepes help keep moisture inside and protect the puff pastry.

4. Take the second part of the puff pastry and put on top to close but be careful not to make a hole in the puff pastry. Paint the puff pastry with egg yolk. To make a nice decorative design on top, run a fork, knife, or other chefs tool in a pattern over top of an extra piece of puff pastry. *Ensure not to puncture the puff pastry when you do this.

5. Place the decoration on top of the puff pastry and brush again with egg yolk.

6. Put in the oven at 350-390 °F (180-200 °C). It is finished when the center of the meat is at the temperature you desire, use the thermometer to check. When ready to serve it is better to cut with a serrated edge knife.

Did you know...

General Wellington is famous because he won the battle of Waterloo bringing to an end Napoleon's reign over France. A new King, friendlier to the English took control of France and the people created a new dish to celebrate. This new dish was named in General Wellington's honor for his contributions towards their new king.

Beef Wellington

TIPS AND TRICKS

After you get coloration on the beef, put aside on a plate to catch the extra liquid (this way the puff pastry can cook better without becoming soggy). If you use a béarnaise sauce, keep it warm in a bain marie until it is ready so that it doesn't break.

ROSIGNY

Mise en place

~1½ lbs (650g) beef filets (4 pieces)
½ lb (200g) foie gras (4 pieces)
4 slices of bread
4 potatoes

Sauce
2 tbsp finely chopped shallots
Port
Stock if available
1⅓ fl. oz (40ml) truffle juice
1½ oz (40g) foie gras

Recipe Difficulty	Level 3
Prep. Time	15 min
Cook Time	20 min
Servings	4
Wine	Burgundy Red or Pinot Noir

LETS GET STARTED...

1. Heat butter in a pan until it is a 'beige/chestnut' color. Salt and pepper the filet, then add to the pan and cook. Ensure to get good coloration on both sides of the filet, and when the beef is cooked as desired, remove and put on a separate plate.

2. Next, start to roast the foie gras at a high temperature in the pan, but then remove to let it cook slowly. If you leave the foie gras in the pan too long it will burn. When ready place on top of the filet of beef.

3. Put bread under the beef, cut in a shape that covers size of beef. The intent of this is to catch any moisture that would come from the beef and ruin your sauce.

Sauce perigourdine:

1. Cook shallots in a pan for 2 or 3 minutes. Next add port and flambé.

2. Next add any juice back from the beef or foie gras, add a little water, add stock (if you had this available), add the additional foie gras that was set aside just for the sauce, the truffle juice, and cook.

3. To finish the sauce, blend to make it smooth using a hand mixer.

4. Works well if you serve with pomme noisette.

Did you know...

Italian musician Rossini initially composed several pieces in Italy including the Barber of Seville before moving to Paris where he composed the William Tell overture, better known as the theme song for the Lone Ranger. He died in 1868.

Rosigny

TIPS AND TRICKS

Keep the beautiful pieces of foie gras for the dish and the smaller or less attractive pieces for the sauce. Remember to keep the sauce that is left from cooking the foie gras to add to the sauce later.

Beef Au Poivre Vert

Mise en place

~1½ lbs (700g) beef filets (4 pieces)
2 tbsp finely chopped shallots
1 tbsp green peppercorns (depending on taste)
Cognac
⅓ cup (80ml) heavy cream
Stock if available

Recipe Difficulty	Level 1
Prep. Time	10 min
Cook Time	15 min
Servings	4
Wine	Bordeaux or Cabernet Sauvignon

Lets Get Started...

1. Heat butter in a pan until it is a 'beige/chestnut' color. Add the filet to the pan and cook. Ensure to get good coloration on both sides of the filet, and when the beef is cooked as desired, remove.

2. Put in an open oven to keep warm (but not cook.)

3. Add butter, shallots into the fry pan. Add green peppers and cognac, and flambé.

4. Add stock, cream, and salt. Add more stock and water if needed. Let the sauce cook slowly so that the pepper has time to work.

5. Pass the sauce through a sieve, blend, and put back on the stove to heat.

6. When ready serve on the dish with 3 or 4 green peppers left for decoration.

Did you know...

In Lyon, named the gastronomical capital of France, you can find a small Roman church in the middle of town. Inside is an interesting tombstone where you will find the body of Mr. Pierre Poivre, famous botanist, who brought pepper back to France in the 18th century. "Poivre" means pepper in French.

Beef au Poivre Vert & Noir

TIPS AND TRICKS

This dish uses "Poivre Vert" which actually means "Green pepper", not to be confused with "Green Bell Pepper", or "Sweet Pepper". You can buy dried green pepper or in a can with juice. If you buy the dry green peppers, put them in water the day before so they can absorb the water and provide a better taste.

BEEF AU POIVRE NOIR

Mise en place

~1½ lbs (700g) beef filets (4 pieces)
*Black peppercorns (see recipe)
⅓ cup (80ml) white wine
¼ cup (55ml) heavy cream
Stock if available

Recipe Difficulty	Level 1
Prep. Time	10 min
Cook Time	15 min
Servings	4
Wine	Bordeaux or Merlot

LETS GET STARTED...

1. Crush large black peppers and cover both sides of the beef. Add salt.

2. Heat butter in a fry pan until it turns beige/hazelnut color. Next add beef and pan sear for color. Remove the meat when cooked as desired, and put in an open oven to keep warm (but not cook.)

3. In the pan you used to roast add white wine and swirl the liquid to remove anything that has stuck to the pan.

4. Add stock, cream, and salt. Add butter and swirl to make a smooth sauce.

5. Add any liquid from the beef in the oven, along with more stock or water if needed.

6. Serve.

Did you know...

There are many different approaches to meat around the world. Many Buddhists are vegetarian and people practicing Hinduism will not eat beef as cows have special religious significance. Be considerate of others beliefs when you choose the dish you will serve.

Beef au Poivre Noir

TIPS AND TRICKS

After you finish cooking your beef, check the color of your butter. If it has started to turn a little black, do not use it as it will make your sauce bitter. It is better to wash the pan and start with new butter.

ROAST VEAL

Mise en place

1⅔ lbs (750g) Veal (filet or thigh)
¼ cup (100g) diced carrot
¼ cup (100g) diced onion
2 cloves garlic
1 sprig thyme & Bay leaf
½ cup (100ml) white wine
Veal stock if available

Recipe Difficulty	Level 1
Prep. Time	10 min
Cook Time	35 min
Servings	4
Wine	Bordeaux or Merlot

LETS GET STARTED...

1. Add salt and pepper on the veal. Choose a pan that is approximately the same size as the veal, and can be used in the stove and in the oven.

2. Heat the pan with oil and butter. When the pan is hot, place the veal inside and sear. You only need a light brown color on the meat at this stage because you will roast in the oven later. Baste the veal in its' own juice while it cooks.

3. Take the pan and place it in the oven and cook at 320 ºF (160 ºC). Add a little fat if you have any empty space in the pan. Don't cover the pan because it will change the color and texture of the meat and your meat will end up being tougher. When finished, remove the meat and any string if you used one.

4. Add cubes of carrot, onion, etc. to the pan with one clove of garlic, thyme, bay leaf and cook for 2 or 3 minutes.

5. Add white wine and swirl to remove any parts stuck to the pan. Cook to reduce the amount of liquid.

6. If you have veal stock, add it to the pan to make a sauce. If you do not have stock, add water, but note that you need to cook longer to reduce the amount of liquid in the pan for more taste. Pass through a sieve and your sauce is ready. If your veal has any juice on the plate put inside the sauce to make tastier.

Did you know...

The meat of a cow is comprised of 65% water, veal 70%. For this reason you start cooking veal with a higher temperature than a cow helping to retain moisture better, and the size of the veal will be better maintained. This also ensures that you keep as much meat as possible for the meal.

Roast Veal

TIPS AND TRICKS

To make the best roast possible, ensure that you place the thermometer in the heart of the meat and not the top or bottom. This ensures when you are checking to see if the meat is cooked appropriately you are measuring the temperature correctly.

DIFFERENT MEAT CUTS

The quality of the beef indicates the texture. For example, type I beef (rump, leg, back) is very tender and can be cooked right away and will taste very good. Type II (sides, ribs, up towards head) needs more time to cook to become tender, and type III (head, bottom legs, ears) takes the longest.

How to cut the meat: Depending on how you cut the meat it ends up either being tender or very tough. Cut down the meat, across the blood vessels that run lengthwise, for better taste.

While the same animal just of a different age, note below the areas of difference for quality in veal.

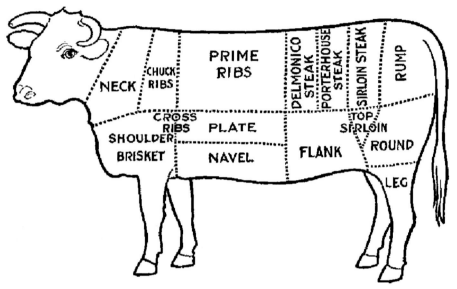

Beef

Here are some temperature guidelines for cooking beef.

"Bleu" or very rare is not cooked at all.
Just warmed

"Saignant" or rare is red with blood inside.
Remove at 136 ºF (58 ºC)

"A point" or medium rare is pink in the middle
Remove at 145 ºF (63 ºC)

Well done, or with no color left inside.
Remove at 158 ºF (70 ºC)

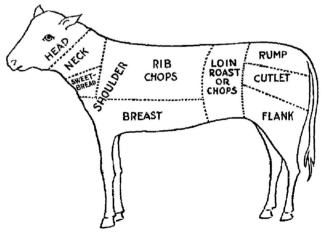

Veal

LAMB

White is meant to represent 'purity' in nearly every known society. Lamb is considered a special animal used symbolically to represent purity because of its white coat. For this reason, you can find many traditions where they kill a lamb on important days to show this faith. In France, the lamb is commonly used as a dish on Easter because of the connection with Christ.

You can find many different religions that refer to the lamb in text or stories. When Abraham was asked to kill his son it was a lamb that was caught and chosen as a replacement, sparing his son and highlighting its relative importance in the world. Symbolically Jesus died for man the way that the lamb died for Abraham. The Christian religion has a special relationship with lamb and that is why it is found often in this faith. Christ is associated with the picture of the lamb, and you will see this symbol found in many different churches commonly portrayed with the famous saying "Jesus is the lamb of God."

There are other famous stories involving lamb, like the Toison d'or that comes from the Greek legend of Jason and the Argonaut. This legend is the origin of a real work when a gold miner killed a lamb and took the fleece with the skin for a coat. This miner then put the fleece in the river, and the very fine pieces of gold flowing in the river stuck inside the fleece of the lamb and made a coat of gold.

Lamb With Fava Beans

Mise en place

1⅔ lbs (750g) lamb thigh (or leg)
3 cloves of garlic
1 sprig thyme
Bay Leaf
½ lb (225g) fava beans

Recipe Difficulty	Level 2
Prep. Time	10 min
Cook Time	30 min
Servings	4
Wine	Bordeaux or Cabernet Sauvignon

Lets Get Started...

1. Slice little holes in the lamb and stuff ½ cloves of garlic inside to cook. Add thyme and bay leaf in the middle of the lamb.

2. Next tie the lamb with string to keep all ingredients inside. *It is important that all these ingredients are inside during cooking so that they don't burn.

3. Add butter in a pan and heat. When the butter is beige/hazelnut color add the lamb and roast to get color but do not cook all the way through.

4. When color is achieved remove and bake in the oven at 355 ºF (180 ºC.)

5. Check the temperature at the center of the meat to know when it's ready based on your taste. Remember to remove when the temperature is 5 ºF (2 ºC) less than you ideally want if you are not going to eat right away.

   Garnish : Boil water with salt and add fava beans. Cook for approximately 5 minutes and when cooked remove the beans and place in cold water. Later, remove the skin around the beans and serve with the lamb.

Did you know...

If you visit the south of France there is a town called Sisteron where you will find the famous 'Agneau du Sisteron'. In this town there are no cows, only a little grass and many herbs. As the animals eat the different herbs the flavor of the herbs eventually permeates through their bodies. In Bretagne, a similar phenomen exists in the 'Agneau du Pre-Salle' (field of salts). In this area the sea has left salt on the land, and when the lamb eats from this field it gives a special taste to the meat.

Lamb with Fava Beans

TIPS AND TRICKS

To make the best leg of lamb, keep it warm for 30 minutes minimum after it has finished cooking and before it is served. This way the color of the meat will be regular throughout.

LAMB BROCHETTES

Mise en place

⅓ lb (150g) thigh of lamb cubed
Bell Peppers cubed (green, red and yellow)
8 rosemary sticks or use regular skewers

Sauce
½ cup (120ml) olive oil
6 finely chopped basil leafs
1 garlic clove

Recipe Difficulty	Level 1
Prep. Time	15 min
Cook Time	15 min
Servings	4
Wine	Languedoc Red or Zinfandel

LETS GET STARTED...

1. Take a piece of lamb and cut it into cubes of approximately the same dimensions.

2. Remove the skin of green, red, and yellow bell peppers using a peeler, and then cut pieces the same size as your cubes of meat. Cook the pieces of bell pepper in boiling water.

3. When ready, mix the cooked bell peppers and lamb on the skewer. *Use a rosemary stick if you have one.

4. Place butter in a hot fry pan and heat. When the butter is a beige/hazelnut color, place the skewer inside and roast.

5. For sauce put olive oil, basil, garlic, salt, and pepper together in a blender and mix.

Did you know...

If you see a lamb in an illustration with a halo around its head then you know it is associated with a religious story. If the lamb is carrying a flag, it is used to show that the resurrection has been accomplished.

Lamb Brochettes

TIPS AND TRICKS

If you want to make a good dish be careful when you start to cook your meat. If your oil/butter is not hot enough, you won't get a good color and the juice will boil in your pan, making your meat tough.

Roasted Lamb Cutlet

Mise en place

4 pieces ~½ lb (200g) of lamb (thigh or filet)
1 sprig thyme
Olive oil

Recipe Difficulty	Level 1
Prep. Time	10 min
Cook Time	10 min
Servings	4
Wine	Bordeaux or Cabernet Sauvignon

Lets Get Started...

1. Add salt and pepper, thyme and a little oil on both sides of thinly sliced or lightly pounded lamb filets.

2. Put on a very hot grill and let it cook. The grill needs to be hot so that the meat does not stick to it.

3. Cook for about 2½ minutes on one side and then turn 45° to get nice grill design marks on the lamb. Cook this way for another 2½ minutes and flip to other side.

4. Use the same 'flip' technique on this side to get nice grill marks but only cook for approximately 1 minute each time.

Did you know...

One patron saint of the chefs is Saint Laurent who lived in the time of the Romans. The Romans told St. Laurent to give money from the church to the emperor but instead, Saint Laurent defied them and gave it to the people. The centurion of the Roman empire took him and to set an example cooked him on a grill. Legend says that when one side of St. Laurent was grilled very well he uttered the words, "Turn me". We hope you don't hear such words from your Paillard D'agneau.

Roasted Lamb Cutlet

TIPS AND TRICKS

Ensure that your filet of lamb is very fine with a flat shape. Use a mallet to flatten your filet before grilling (cover with plastic wrap before hitting the meat.)

CURRIED LAMB STEW

Mise en place

1¾ lbs (800g) thigh of lamb (large cubes)
¼ lb (100g) cubed onion
¼ lb (100g) tomato (peeled, seeded & diced)
½ cup (100ml) white wine
Curry for taste

2 apples *Granny Smith
Sugar
2 bananas
Butter

Recipe Difficulty	Level 1
Prep. Time	15 min
Cook Time	60 min
Servings	4
Wine	Bordeaux or Cabernet Sauvignon

LETS GET STARTED...

1. Place butter in a hot fry pan and heat. When the butter is a beige/hazelnut color, sprinkle the lamb with salt and pepper and place in the pan to roast. When the lamb has a good color on all sides remove and put on a plate.

2. In the pan where you cooked the lamb, add onion and tomato to the pan and cook. Add white wine and swirl to remove anything that has stuck to the pan. Cook to remove the alcohol and reduce the amount of liquid in the pan. Next add water and then cook at a slow boil to reduce the volume of liquid.

3. Add curry powder to your taste, add the lamb, and then cook all together for 45 minutes. If there is not enough sauce, or if it is too thin, add a roux of oil and flour.

4. Put the lamb on a plate and pour the sauce through a sieve.

Garnish:

1. Remove the core and seeds of the apple and slice into ~1/2 inch (1cm) thick circles. Heat a different pan with sugar inside. Once caramelizing starts, add a little fresh butter inside and mix/swirl. Place these slices in the pan and add water to the same level of the apples. Cook until no water is left. When you see the caramel appear again the apples are ready. When you serve with the lamb, turn the apples so that the shiny part is on top.

2. Take slices of banana and roast in butter. Add to the lamb when ready.

3. *If you want, you can add cooked circles of carrot in the middle of the apple slices.

Did you know...

In the Greek and Roman cultures the divine were women priests that were mediums for consulting with the gods. They used different animals to create oracles to predict the future, however it was believed that the cleaner the animal the better the predictions. To create this oracle, they sacrifice a lamb, and then view the organs inside for positive signs to proceed.

Curried Lamb Stew

TIPS AND TRICKS

Normally, you go to the butcher and buy "navarin d'agneau" for this recipe, which comes from the 2nd or 3rd category quality of meat. If you don't have a lot of time, you can use the leg or other first quality meats as it will tenderize quicker.

LAMB & PORK

When you make lamb, you want to have a good color on the outside, pink on the inside. Cook very fast at first to get color and then reduce the temperature to cook very slowly to let the inside cook properly. Let the meat sit aside for a few minutes before serving.

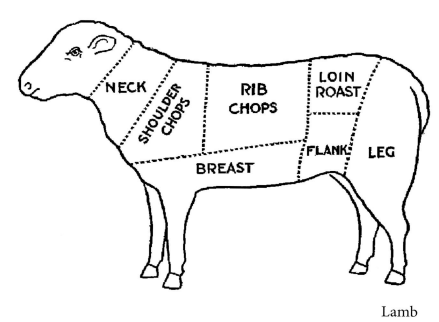

Lamb

Mr Brillat-Savarin has said that the quality of the dish is equal to the quality of the product. The better quality product you buy, the better your end result.

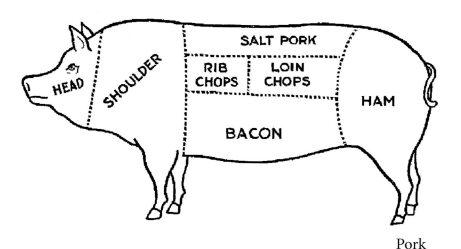

Pork

PORK

Before the invention of electricity there was no refrigerator or means of transportation, so when planning for food it was necessary to depend on the seasons. During the winter in France, it was possible to find some fruit and

Pork, however, responds very well to salt and the taste of pork is commonly enhanced with salt. Therefore, pork was most often the meat chosen. For this reason you will find many illustrations in very old calendars o r

churches illustrating that pork is taken and prepared in early winter. Above (center) you will find an example of a stained glass window you could encounter.

vegetables that you could keep, however the meat was more difficult. Salts were used to help preserve meat through the winter, but unfortunately, salt also cooks many different kinds of meat.

PORK CHOPS

Mise en place

4 pieces of ¾ lbs (170g) Pork
¼ cup (50g) butter
Pinch of garlic
1 sprig thyme
3 ladles of stock if available

Recipe Difficulty	Level 1
Prep. Time	10 min
Cook Time	10 min
Servings	4
Wine	Languedoc Red or Zinfandel

LETS GET STARTED...

1. Heat a pan with oil. When you see the first smoke in the pan you can add the pork and roast. When the pork has good color on both sides, remove from the pan.

2. To make the sauce, add butter, garlic, salt, pepper and the thyme to the same pan and cook until it achieves a beige/hazelnut color.

3. If you want to make a better sauce, add ladles of stock to the pan, and cook to reduce the volume of liquid to make it thicker.

*It is better to have a thicker piece of pork for this recipe and you can serve this dish with any sauce you like. **Pork Chops "Côte de porc" can also be and served with head waiter (see basics) or a compound butter.

Did you know...

Pork and its use are very contested in different parts of the world. Many countries have a bad image of this animal because it lives in the dirt and mud etc. For this reason, some religions tell their followers not to eat pork because it is not clean or pure.

Pork Chops

TIPS AND TRICKS

If you have never tried cote de pork from a farmer, try it and you should be pleasantly surprised at the quality and taste. It is important to get a piece of pork that is thick enough so that enough juice is kept inside to remain tender.

PORK "NORMANDY STYLE"

Mise en place

1⅓ lbs (600g) thinly sliced pork
2 tbsp finely chopped shallots
¼ cup (60ml) white wine
⅔ lb (300g) sliced mushrooms
*3 ladles of stock if you have
⅓ cup (80ml) heavy cream

Recipe Difficulty	Level 1
Prep. Time	15 min
Cook Time	30 min
Servings	4
Wine	Beaujolais Red or Pinot Noir

LETS GET STARTED...

1. Place butter in a hot pan and heat. When the butter is a beige/hazelnut color place the pork inside and roast. Remove the pork when finished and put on a plate to the side.

2. Sweat mushrooms in the same pan where the pork was roasted. Get a good color on the mushrooms. Add shallots, salt and pepper.

3. Add white wine and swirl to remove anything that has stuck to the pan.

4. Add cream and swirl to make a thick and consistent sauce.

5. Add any juice that you find on the plate with the pork. Add a little first, mix, and then add the rest. This helps to keep the consistency of your sauce from breaking.

6. Add back the pork to warm a little before serving.

7. For a nice garnish, serve with roosti with bacon. *Boil the cube of bacon then roast before adding to roosti for a better taste.

Did you know...

Normandy is a region in France invaded by the Vikings over and over again. To end these invasions the French king decided to just give the region to the Vikings. When you translate Norman in French it means Viking. There are many cows in Normandy. This recipe contains crème from the cow which is why it is called 'a la Normande'.

Pork "Normandy" style

TIPS AND TRICKS

When you have finished getting good color on the meat, remove and set aside while you make your sauce. When your sauce is finished, add the meat back inside to help keep tender.

FROG LEGS WITH ASPARAGUS

Mise en place

1⅓ lbs (600g) frogs (grenouilles)
4 kebab sticks
20 asparagus heads
Flour
Salt
Pepper

Recipe Difficulty	Level 1
Prep. Time	20 min
Cook Time	15 min
Servings	4
Wine	Pessac-Léognan or Semillon

LETS GET STARTED...

1. Remove the fingers and the front bones of the frogs with scissors. Take the meat, add salt and pepper, and then skewer on a kebab.

2. Mix together flour, water, salt and pepper. Roll the kebabs in this mix.

3. Heat a pan with oil and when you see the first smoke place the kebabs inside. Baste in their own juices frequently until you achieve a good color.

4. Heat another pan, and when the butter is beige/hazelnut color, add the asparagus and roast for 2 minutes.

5. Serve the kebab on top of the asparagus.

Did you know...

The English commonly call the French "Frogs" for a joke. Of course it is true that the French eat frogs and the most famous region to find these frogs is Dombe. If you visit this small region you will find every restaurant there offers at least one dish with frogs. The other dishes commonly served in this region incorporate river fish.

Frog Legs with asparagus

TIPS AND TRICKS

If you can't find fresh frogs, it is better to skip this dish. Try an authentic version of this dish when you next visit France.

FROGS PERSILLADE

Mise en place

1¾ lbs (800g) frogs (grenouilles)
1 tbsp finely chopped garlic
1½ tbsp finely chopped parsley
Lemon for taste

Recipe Difficulty	Level 1
Prep. Time	10 min
Cook Time	15 min
Servings	4
Wine	Alsace Pinot Gris or Pinot Gris

LETS GET STARTED...

1. Remove the fingers and the front bones of the frogs with scissors.

2. Place butter in a hot pan and heat. When the butter is a beige/hazelnut color place the frogs inside and roast. Baste with their own juices frequently so that the meat does not get dry.

3. Achieve a good color on the meat and then add chopped garlic and parsley (add parsley at the very end so it doesn't turn black). Add lemon for taste.

Did you know...

The toad is found in many different stories and legends. In some, the toad is symbolic to show that one should not look solely at appearances, but to find what is really inside, like the princess who kissed the toad to find her prince.

Frogs Persillade

TIPS AND TRICKS

Put your parsley in the dish at the last minute because the heat and the lemon will make the parsley black.

POTATOES

Unfortunately for the potato, they were forbidden in 1630 by the Kings' doctors because they were thought to cause the plague

Potatoes arrived in 1534 from South America before having this unfortunate association wth the plague. While we know today potatoes were not the cause, it was Mr. Parmentier in 1770 who fought to have the potatoes reintroduced in France. Legend says that Parmentier buried them in the ground and then had them guarded all day in front of all the people. At night he let the guards leave so that there was a chance for the potatoes to be stolen. Of course the potatoes were subsequently stolen and then spread throughout the country, where they were now grown by the people.

At first the use of potatoes spread very slowly, but 19 years later (1789) a revolution started against the king because of a famine. The revolution ended when the people beheaded the king, but there was still no food to eat. At this time, the new government decided to use the potatoes now found throughout France as a food to fight the famine. Not all people cheered the revolution and killing of the king. The people in the Vendee region called the potatoes the "Apple of the Devil" because they came from the men of the revolution who had killed the king that they were friendly to.

Pictorial during the revolution for food

ROSTI

Mise en place

1¾ lbs (800g) potatoes
 *New potatoes are better

Recipe Difficulty	Level 2
Prep. Time	5 min
Cook Time	35 min
Servings	4
Wine	match with the main dish

1. Bring a pot of water to boil. Add potatoes and cook in the skin until just before they are ready (75% finished.)

2. Remove, peel potatoes and then shred/grate. Add salt and pepper for taste. Preheat a pan with butter to a moderate heat and add the potatoes inside. Press the potatoes flat and round edges to make it look like a pie and cook.

3. When you have good color on one side, flip the whole thing like a crepe.

TIPS AND TRICKS

You can add onion, ham, garlic, or anything you like to this recipe to cook with the potatoes. Add these ingredients just after the potatoes are peeled.

Did you know...

Switzerland is considered a federation of 3 states that have existed for ~800 years. The last region to join the federation was French and has been a member for just over 100 years. Bern has been a member of the Swiss federation since 1353 and is a region famous for Rosti.

Rosti

GRATIN DAUPHINOIS

Mise en place

1⅔ lbs (750g) potatoes (before peeling)
3 cups (725ml) whole milk
1 tbsp finely chopped garlic
1½ tbsp (20g) butter
1½ cups (375ml) heavy cream
½ cup (100g) shredded Gruyere cheese

Recipe Difficulty	Level 1
Prep. Time	15 min
Cook Time	90 min
Servings	6
Wine	match with the main dish

LETS GET STARTED...

1. Wash, peel, and then slice potatoes thin. After slicing the potatoes do not wash them because you want the starch to remain in the potato.

2. In a pan heated with warm butter add garlic and milk and bring to a boil.

3. Next add potatoes, salt and pepper if you want. Mix to ensure the potatoes do not burn and slowly boil. Ensure that the liquid is completely covering the potatoes through the entire process.

4. The potatoes are ready when you can put a knife in and remove cleanly.

5. Add salt and pepper for taste and cream to finish.

6. Put in a dish and sprinkle cheese on top.

7. Broil to get a nice brown color on top to finish.

*You can put in the fridge until you need it, but if you do, broil just before serving.

Did you know...

Gratin Dauphinois comes from the Dauphin region located near the Savoy. This recipe was created and named because the heir apparent to the king, 'dauphin' in French, was in charge of this region. The symbol of this region is the dolphin, the other meaning for "Dauphin."

Gratin Dauphinois

TIPS AND TRICKS

If you like nutmeg, adding a little when you cook can create a very good flavor. If you want to make the plate more pleasing, put a circle in the pan and lift underneath with a spatula; this will allow your serving to have a nice form.

Pomme 'Maxim' Potato

Mise en place

Garnish and Decoration
1lb (450g) cups potatoes
6½ tbsp (90g) butter
Flour
Wax paper

Recipe Difficulty	Level 2
Prep. Time	15 min
Cook Time	30 min
Servings	4
Wine	match with the main dish

Lets Get Started...

1. Put a hollow circle through a potato to get a circle shaped piece of potato.

2. Use a mandolin to slice the round piece of potato so that all pieces are similar.

3. Put in cold water and boil once.

4. Dissolve butter and brush on top of potatoes, and then add flour.

5. Draw a circle on a leaf of wax paper with pen and then turn the paper over.

6. Layer the potato pieces in a circle pattern around edge of circle.

7. Brush potato again with butter, add salt and pepper, and put on a baking tray. Add another leaf of wax paper on top and then lay another baking tray on top so the potatoes don't move.

8. Cook at 320 ºF (160 ºC) until brown.

Did you know...

Maxim is the name of a famous restaurant in Paris. The reputation of this restaurant became strong enough to become a common phrase. Maxim is now sometimes used to say a dinner is very good,. "Oh la la le diner c'est Maxim!"...

Pomme "Maxim"

TIPS AND TRICKS

Make sure to add the salt after cooking because the potatoes cook better this way.

'Sure To Please' Potatoes

Mise en place

Saute a Cru
1¾ lbs (800g) potatoes (not peeled)
1 sprig thyme
Bay leaf
*Onion thinly sliced (optional)

Saute coin de rue
1¾ lbs (800g) potatoes
1 sprig thyme
Bay leaf
2 cloves of garlic

Potatoes "Noisette"
1¾ lbs (800g) potatoes

Recipe Difficulty	Level 1
Prep. Time	10 min
Cook Time	20-35 min
Servings	4
Wine	match with the main dish

Potatoes "Noisette"

1. Peel an uncooked potato and make little balls with a melon-ball tool.

2. Put potato balls in a pan with cold water and boil for 1 minute.

3. Remove, and then roast in fry pan with butter. The potato balls should have good color and be tender.

Potatoes "A Cru"

1. Peel, and then slice potatoes ~¼ inch/ 5mm width using a mandoline. Wash potatoes after slicing to remove the starch. Use a strainer if you find it easier.

2. Put oil and butter in hot pan (but not too hot). If the pan is too cold the potatoes will stick. Add thyme and bay leaf and then flip the potatoes until done.

3. *If you want to make "Pomme de terre a Lyonnaise" add thinly sliced onion when almost finished and then cook for 5 minutes.

Potatoes "Coin De Rue"

1. Peel potatoes and cut in cubes of ½ inch / 1cm. Place in cold water and bring to a boil and then remove the potatoes.

2. Heat a frying pan with oil and a little butter. Add the potatoes, thyme, bay leaf, and garlic and cook to get good color. When finished add salt for taste.

Did you know...

Potatoes contain a starch that is similar to flour. You can use this starch mixed with water to make a sauce thicker. It can actually create a shining sauce, but this liaison is not as stable as others. The French name for the 'saute' potatoes are from a time when streets were made of cobblestone. Cobblestone, first used by the Romans is now typically used only for pedestrian streets. In cycling's Tour de France there is a famous leg at Compiègne where the Paris-Roubaix race starts. Here cyclists need to pass over a cobblestone street and if you can imagine, this just might be the worst part for the riders.

Potato Possibilities

TIPS AND TRICKS

If you can find them, use fingerling potatoes for "a cru" and "coin de rue" because of their excellent taste. Don't peel but wash them very well. New potatoes and waxy potatoes have lower starch content than the mature potatoes (e.g. Rousset/Idaho). For "noisette" can also cut into cubes. To save you 5 to 10 minutes, never add salt when you start as they will cook quicker. Use new (young) potatoes for this recipe.

FRIES "PONT NEUF"

Mise en place

1¾ lbs (800g) potatoes
Vegetable oil

Recipe Difficulty	Level 1
Prep. Time	15 min
Cook Time	20 min
Servings	4
Wine	match with the main dish

LETS GET STARTED...

1. Fill a pot no more (maximum) than ¾ full with vegetable oil. Heat the vegetable oil to 285 ºF (140 ºC.)

2. Cut the potatoes into 'fries' shape ~½ inch (1cm) cubed by ~3 inches (7cm) long.

3. Cook once and remove from the oil. When they feel a little soft with your fingers they are ready.

4. Now heat the pot with oil to 355 ºF (180 ºC). Put the potatoes back in the oil to finish. This last step helps to make the potatoes crispy.

Did you know...

When you build a bridge ("pont" in French) you use scaffolding. The form of this dish is presented in the same shape as the scaffolding you would find around bridges. This presentation is the very classic form of this dish and when done in this manner you can call it "Pomme Pont Neuf."

Pont Neuf (Bridge)

TIPS AND TRICKS

Wash the potatoes after cutting to remove the starch from the potatoes. This will help them to not stick when you fry.

BAKED POTATO

Mise en place

Four ~½ lb (225g) potatoes
Coarse Salt, Aluminium foil

Sauce
⅔ cups (160ml) heavy cream
3 tbsp finely chopped chives
Lemon juice for taste

Recipe Difficulty	Level 2
Prep. Time	15 min
Cook Time	35 min
Servings	4
Wine	match with the main dish

1. Add salt to the bottom of the pan to keep the potatoes from burning. Wash the potatoes and wrap each separately in aluminum foil.

2. Put in an oven at 320 °F (160 °C). When you can put a knife inside the potato and remove cleanly it is ready. You do not need to open the aluminum foil to check this.

3. Sauce – Whisk cream together with salt, pepper and chives. Add lemon, continue to whisk, and it will thicken.

4. To serve the potato make a cut lengthwise, squeeze the sides to open a bit more, add the sauce inside with a small spoon.

TIPS AND TRICKS

It is a better to serve this potato with a 'country' style meal. Country style often means large portions and a good taste are more important than an intricate presentation.

Baked Potato "mise en place"

Did you know...

Potato BF (Belle de Fontenay) 15 was introduced in France in 1885. It's used because it keeps a better potato shape and has a crisper texture. If you want a smooth texture, it is better to use a Bintje potato (introduced in 1910). The Bintje potato is best if you want to cook for a long time and the shape is not as important.

PASTA

Did pasta originate in China, Italy or somewhere else?

People constantly fight over the origins of pasta. For most Europeans Italian pasta is more recognized and thought to be the original. In France, it was Catherine Medeci of Italy who brought the technique of making pasta when she married King Henri II and made it popular in France. This pasta was made from wheat. Most people have heard about this origin of pasta, but are not familiar with the origin of pasta in China. In the 13th century, travelers such as Marco Polo found their way to China and discovered various foods, one of them being pasta made from rice. Now you know when people fight over the country of the origin of pasta you can tell them that pasta is made two different ways, and that they both could be right.

NOODLES

Mise en place

3¼ cups (400g) flour
3 large (200g) eggs
2½ tbsp olive oil

Recipe Difficulty	Level 1
Prep. Time	40 min
Cook Time	3 min
Servings	4
Wine	Pair with the main dish, otherwise, with the sauce

LETS GET STARTED...

1. You can add various colors to the pasta if you like:

   - Green - you can use spinach chopped very fine, or chlorophyll
   - Red - you can use tomato concentrate or a concasse de tomate
   - Black - packages of squid ink or a yellow curry powder

2. Put flour in the bowl in a circle shape leaving a hole in the middle. Put the eggs in that hole and use your finger to break the egg. If you add any color or flavouring do it now and mix only with the egg in the middle.

3. You don't want to make a ball so try not to press the ingredients together. Mix the liquid and the flour together very well and when they are fully mixed then press together and make dough shaped more like a ball.

4. Now knead the dough using strong hands but don't work for too long. The less you work the better, this way the dough will not be too elastic. Add flour or water as you need to get the right dough consistency.

5. Next work the dough with a rolling pin or pasta machine to make even and thin. When ready put through a pasta machine to make the shape that you want.

6. Allow the pasta to dry by resting 10 minutes minimum, where it can hang freely. Cook in boiling water with salt and olive oil for 3 minutes.

7. To make multicoloured dough: put all pieces of different colors on top of each other, slice and put together in an alternating pattern. Then work the dough to form a new dough so that colors are mixed.

Did you know...

Nouille is the name for these noodles used in France, but in Italy it has a different name which is called "Tagliatelle". This pasta is usually very good when used fresh and has an uncanny ability to taste great with nearly any sauce that you pair it with.

Noodles

TIPS AND TRICKS

If you added salt inside the flour and eggs, you may have white specs in your pasta when it has dried. It is better to add the salt after you have cooked.

SPATZLE

Mise en place

2⅔ cups (330g) flour
3 eggs
½ cup (100ml) water
½ cup (100ml) milk
½ tbsp dill
3 caps of oil

*6 tbsp of tomato concasse (see basics)

Recipe Difficulty	Level 2
Prep. Time	15 min
Cook Time	15 min
Servings	4
Wine	Pair with the main dish, otherwise, with the sauce

LETS GET STARTED...

1. Mix together all ingredients in a bowl with salt and pepper for taste.

2. Using a metal screen with ~ ½ inch / 9mm size holes (or other equipment you may have), push the dough through the holes into boiling water. When the pieces are ready they will float on top of the water.

3. Heat a little butter in a pan. When hot, add pieces of pasta and cook to make crispy. Ensure to not let the pieces stick to the pan.

   *Optionally, add a little tomato concasse as a sauce.

Did you know...

The origin of this dough comes from the east of France, popular in Alsace, a region bordering Germany. Spatzli is traditionally used with dishes containing game, served in the winter. The pronunciation itself can show you it is not of traditional French origin.

Spatzle

TIPS AND TRICKS

If you want to make a good Spatzle, remove the pieces as soon as they rise to the top or they will become sticky with a soft texture.

RAVIOLI

Mise en place

1¾ cups (225g) flour
2 (110g) eggs

1 lb (450g) rock shrimp (langoustine)
2 tbsp finely chopped shallots
2 tbsp olive oil
*small herbs i.e. parsley

Recipe Difficulty	Level 2
Prep. Time	30 min
Cook Time	3 min
Servings	4
Wine	Pair with the main dish, otherwise, with the sauce

LETS GET STARTED...

1. Put flour in a bowl in a circle shape leaving a hole in the middle. Put the eggs in that hole and using your finger break the eggs and mix together.

2. Try not to press the ingredients together as you don't want to make a ball of dough. Mix the liquid and the flour together and once they are fully mixed now press together and make dough shaped more like a ball.

3. Knead the dough but not for very long. The less you knead the better, this way the dough will not be too elastic. Add flour or water as needed to get the right dough consistency. Place in the fridge while you make the filling.

Langoustine / Rock Shrimp Filling:

1. Take off the tails of the rock shrimp which is where you will find the meat. Wiggle the covering back and forth to remove the shell that is on the tail to get the meat.

2. Fry in a pan with shallots, salt and pepper. Cut into small pieces and mix with shallots and any other small herbs that you like.

3. Take the dough from the fridge and roll out thin. Cut holes in the dough using either round forms or special ravioli trays (dust with flour first). Put the filling on the dough and brush with water on the outside.

4. Finish the ravioli by putting another layer of dough on top and cut larger pieces of dough than initially so that you ensure the ravioli will completely seal. Put in boiling water with salt and olive oil to cook.

  *Note that when using forms leave the top form bigger than the bottom form because it has to cover the bottom form and all the filling.

Did you know...

Italy is an ancient country with a long history of culture derived from the Romans. This culture and cuisine came to France with the Romans and have given the name of one of the first architectural styles "Roman". The famous French chef hat seen in many pictures may actually have originated from Italy. Its interesting how it has changed in various regions, in France, it is more upright, and in Italy a little more flat.

Ravioli

TIPS AND TRICKS

Choosing what to stuff your ravioli with is only limited by your imagination. If you make large ravioli, cook in a steamer so that the ravioli does not break from the filling.

Noodles With Morels

Mise en place

1⅓ lb (600g) noodles
1½ oz (40g) dry morel mushrooms
2 tbsp finely chopped shallots
Cognac
Morel juice
⅓ cup (80ml) heavy cream

Recipe Difficulty	Level 1
Prep. Time	15 min
Cook Time	15 min
Servings	4
Wine	Pair with the main dish, otherwise, with the sauce

Lets Get Started...

1. If you use dehydrated morels, soak the morels in hot water to rehydrate, and keep the water you soak them in for later.

2. Heat a little butter in a pan. Roughly chop the morels and place in the pan. Add shallots, cognac and then flambé.

3. Next add the morel juice from earlier except for the very last part as it can contain dirt fragments.

4. Add cream, salt and pepper. Boil together and cook until it becomes a nice texture for a sauce.

5. Serve with noodles (see earlier recipe.)

Did you know...

Monera, Protista, Plantae, Fungi and Animalia were considered the 5 kingdoms by Whittaker. The fungi kingdom was broken out from Protista which contain mushrooms, a special vegetal that have various types and no chlorophyll. For pasta it is better to use one of the higher quality mushrooms from the mushroom family because they are tastier. Bolete, chantrelle, or morel mushrooms are recommended for this reason.

Noodles with Morels

TIPS AND TRICKS

If you buy dry morels, put them first in warm water to saturate. Save the water from which they are removed and use later for your sauce. Never add the last part though because there may be some dirt or stones.

DESSERTS

Desserts are associated with the good times in ones life because they are nearly always used for moments of celebration. Most of the classic cakes are in the shape of a circle, because within a circle all of the people can look at the same instant and symbolically see the same thing, have the same 'cut' (piece) and therefore equally share in the celebration. Others believe it was round because of the association with celebration for the moon Goddess, candles representing the light of the moon. In any case, desserts are exceptionally special because they are associated with an elated emotion. You are sure to remember the dessert from your birthday or marriage. For these events there is an association of the dessert and an important time of your life.

It is interesting to note one of the first tastes you experience and enjoy as a baby is sugar, as well as it being one of the last you are capable to enjoy. We hope you keep this nice taste throughout your entire life.

Red Fruit "Soupe"

Mise en place

1 cup (220ml) water
½ cup (110g) sugar
1¼ lb (550g) red fruits

Recipe Difficulty	Level 1
Prep. Time	15 min
Cook Time	1 hr refrigerated
Servings	4
Wine	Sautérnes or Muscat

1. Put water in a pan and add sugar. Dissolve slowly by heating. Pour directly over fruits in a bowl and put in the fridge for one hour minimum before serving.

Red Fruit "Soupe"

TIPS AND TRICKS

Remember to wash your red fruits well as you will eat them directly. If you want to have the best taste, marinade for 3 hours minimum before serving.

Did you know...

One component of the strawberry is salicylic acid which is used in many skin care products, can reduce fever, and is a component of aspirin. The salicylic acid is one reason if you have problems with your teeth you can eat strawberries and it's not so bad.

CRÈME CARAMEL

Mise en place

4 cups (1L) milk
6 eggs
¾ cup (150g) sugar, sifted
1 vanilla bean

Caramel
½ cup (100g) sugar
½ cup (100ml) water

Recipe Difficulty	Level 1
Prep. Time	15 min
Cook Time	20 min +1 day
Servings	12
Wine	Sautérnes, Muscat or Champagne

LETS GET STARTED...

1. Have the baking forms that you plan to use for the crème caramel ready.

2. Cut the vanilla bean in two, scrape the black pieces into the pot with the milk and bring to a boil. After the milk has boiled remove from the heat.

3. In another pan, make caramel using 50% sugar and 50% water. Add water to the pan, then the sugar and heat. Wait for the color to change and when it does you need to move quickly.

4. Pour this caramel into the base of the shapes you have chosen as soon as it is ready. Caramel is used for taste and also ensures that the crème caramel won't stick to the form.

5. Mix eggs with sugar to dissolve the sugar and then mix with milk/vanilla combination. Do not add the eggs/sugar mix too quickly because you could cook your eggs if the milk/vanilla mixture has not cooled sufficiently.

6. When all ingredients are mixed, pour into the chosen shapes (on top of the caramel) and bake in the oven at 250 °F (120 °C) for 20 minutes minimum. It's ready when you can slide a normal knife in and remove cleanly.

Did you know...

The establishment of sugar capability in Europe occurred when Napoleon was the emperor of France. During the Napoleonic wars there was a time when the boats from England were blocked and therefore could not arrive with sugarcane. It was this event that led to the discovery of sugar extraction from beets that reduced the cost and increased the production quantity allowing for great inventions and leaps in uses of sugar.

Crème Caramel

TIPS AND TRICKS

Fresh vanilla from vanilla sticks provides the best taste. Make one day prior to serving so that the caramel has a chance to dissolve.

CRÈME BRULE

Mise en place

9 (180g) egg yolks
⅓ cup (75g) sugar, sifted
2⅔ cups (665ml) heavy cream
½ cup (110ml) milk
Flavouring

Recipe Difficulty	Level 1
Prep. Time	10 min
Cook Time	45 min + 1 day
Servings	10
Wine	Sautérnes, Muscat or Champagne

LETS GET STARTED...

1. *Note for this recipe you can add anything you want for flavour (coffee, vanilla, etc) but you have to add it to the milk. Add the milk and cream together, bring to a boil, and then let cool.

2. Mix the egg yolk and the sugar together and then mix into the milk/crème solution.

3. Pour into the shapes that you have chosen and bake at 250 ºF (120 ºC) for approximately 40 minutes. It's ready when you can slide a normal knife in and remove cleanly.

4. Once cooked remove and sift brown sugar on top. Make sure to keep the sides of the dish clean. Use a torch to lightly burn the sugar and get a nice coloration on the top.

5. If you do not have a torch, a salamander broiler is best, otherwise try using the oven broiler although the end result may not look as perfect. Adjust the racks to be 2" away from the broiler and preheat for 10 minutes before putting them in the oven. With the crème brule on a baking tray place under the broiler. It will be ready when the sugar bubbles and melts.

Did you know...

As a patisserie there are great rewards in making a good dessert. However, there is also more pressure because you are always working for a special occasion reflecting an important moment in someone's life. Wanting to create something special and good feelings for these moments is why the patisserie works so hard to ensure the result is always good.

Crème Brule

TIPS AND TRICKS

If you use your personal oven you need to have a very hot broiler to burn the top, a better option is to use a portable torch. A sift is better to use when sprinkling the brown sugar on top as it ensures it is spread evenly and eliminates the chance for undesirable lumps.

TARTE TATIN

Mise en place

½ lb (250g) Pâté Feuilletée (basics)
8 apples
½ cup (100g) sugar
½ cup (100ml) water
Butter
Apricot jelly

*You can use Pâté Sucrée instead of Pâté Feuilletée
but the latter is better.

Recipe Difficulty	Level 2
Prep. Time	15 min
Cook Time	25 min
Servings	8
Wine	Cider, Sautérnes or Muscat

LETS GET STARTED...

1. Put the tip of your peeler into the apple near the core until your thumb touches. Then turn around the rim and it will allow you to remove the stem/core. You may need to repeat this step to be successful. Next peel the apples.

2. Cut the apple in two and remove any middle core or seeds that you find and then slice the apples into 6ths or 8ths.

3. *If you want to caramelize the apples, put water with sugar in a skillet and cook. When the sugar turns a brown color add a little butter and swirl the pan. Add the apples and cook.

4. Use a fork to make little holes in the bottom of the Pâté Feuilletée. Then place the Pâté Feuilletée in the oven at 355 ºF (180 ºC). It is ready when the dough is a good brown color. This should take approximately 10-15 minutes. Use a circle or pie form to cut the Pâté Feuilletée. Tear away any extra dough.

5. Next put down the circle form (not the dough) on top of a piece of plastic wrap, and put apples inside so that there are no holes and looks very beautiful.

6. Put the dough on top of the apples, inside the circle. Then by grabbing the plastic wrap tightly with the bottom, flip on to a plate.

7. Dissolve apricot jelly over heat and then brush the top of the tarte tatin to make shiny.

Did you know...

Tatin is a recipe that comes from 2 sisters in France. Legend says that the sisters made a beautiful tarte, but then slipped and fell causing the tarte to turn upside down with the dough on top. Since this time people have kept this idea and now all tartes are made with dough on top. This dish tastes very good warm, with a scoop of vanilla ice cream on the side.

Technique to prepare Tarte Tatin

Tarte Tatin

TIPS AND TRICKS

If possible, find a special copper mold to make this dish as the copper retains the heat better and does not burn the tarte as easily. *you can use pate sucree instead of pate feuillete, but pate feuillette is better.

APPLE TART

Mise en place

½ lb (250g) Pâté Feuilletée (basics)
4 apples
3 tbsp sugar
Butter
Apricot jelly

*You can use Pâté Sucrée or Pate Brisee instead of Pâté Feuilletée but the latter is better.

Recipe Difficulty	Level 1
Prep. Time	15 min
Cook Time	20 min
Servings	6
Wine	Cider, Sautérnes or Muscat

LETS GET STARTED...

1. Put the tip of your peeler into the apple near the core until your thumb touches. Then turn around the rim and it will allow you to remove the stem/core. You may need to repeat this step to be successful. Next peel the apples.

2. Cut the apple in two and remove any middle core or seeds that you find.

3. After you have removed all of the seeds cut the apples into thin slices for the top of the pie.

4. Put a hollow circle form on the baking tray and butter where the circle is. Sprinkle sugar on top of the butter as it adds taste to pie. Cut out dough into the circle shape and move it to the baking tray. Use a fork to make little holes in the bottom of the Pâté Feuilletae (puff pastry).

5. Using a spatula or other flat tool so that it doesn't break, place the slices of apples on top of the dough in a circular direction. Place all in the same direction to make it look more beautiful.

6. Brush the apples with butter, sprinkle sugar, and put in the oven at 355 °F (180 °C) for approximately 20 minutes. Check the bottom of the dough to see if it is brown. When the bottom is a good brown color it is ready.

7. Spread a little oil on a cold surface and put the tarte au pommes there first, and then on a plate.

8. Dissolve apricot jelly over heat and then brush on top of the apple tart to make it shine. Let cool for 10-20 minutes minimum before serving.

Did you know...

Apple cider tastes great with the tarte aux pommes. The region considered to be the 'country of the apple' is Normandy which can be found near famous Mont St. Michel. In this region you will find the greatest variety of apples, and is known to have some of the best cider in France.

Adam and Eve

TIPS AND TRICKS

When you have finished cooking the tarte aux pommes, you will find caramel under your dough. Ideally you should move quickly and remove the tarte putting it on a cold surface already covered with butter or oil so it doesn't stick.

CHOCOLATE MOUSSE

Mise en place

(a) ⅓ lb (160g) 55% chocolate
(b) 3 egg yolk & 1½ tbsp (20g) sugar, sifted
(c) 3 egg whites & 1¼ tbsp (15g) sugar
(d) ¾ cups (200ml) heavy cream

Recipe Difficulty	Level 2
Prep. Time	10 min (+ 1 hr)
Cook Time	20 min
Servings	6
Wine	Sautérnes or Muscat

LETS GET STARTED...

1. First whisk the (b) egg yolks with the 1½ tbsp sugar until it achieves a creamy texture with a cream color.

2. In a separate bowl whisk the (c) egg whites with 1 tbsp of sugar until it has a thick texture.

3. In a third bowl whisk (d) the cream until it becomes thick. When you can turn the bowl upside down and the cream doesn't move it's ready. *It is better if you can whisk in an area with cold air to help keep the white color.

4. Bring a pot of water to a slow boil. Then place (a) the chocolate in another bowl and place over top of the pot of water so that the heat and steam from the pot of water melt the chocolate. Use a spatula/marise to help dissolve the chocolate.

5. Next add (a) the chocolate with the (b) egg yolk and sugar mixture and stir quickly, otherwise the chocolate will harden and it will be impossible to use. Then add a little chocolate to (d) the whipped cream and turn the cream over top using a spatula. Repeat this process until all the chocolate has been mixed throughout. You need to add this chocolate in 2 or 3 separate steps to be successful.

6. Next using a spatula slowly fold in (c) the egg whites and sugar to the chocolate mix.

7. Pour in a form and refrigerate for 1 hour minimum before serving.

Did you know...

In the dictionary you can find a word that comes from the language of the Maya people from South America, chocolate, which they derived from the cacao bean. The conquistadors kept this name and integrated it into the everyday language of Portugese, French, Spanish etc.

Chocolate Mousse

TIPS AND TRICKS

When you dissolve your chocolate be sure to not have even one drop of water in with the chocolate. Chocolate and water become a stone texture when mixed together making it impossible to use with other ingredients.

STRAWBERRY DESSERT CAKE

Mise en place

1 piece of biscuit (see basics)
Plastic wrap
2 (50g) egg whites
¾ cups (200ml) heavy cream
3 leafs of gelatin
¼ lb (100g) strawberries
¾ cups (200ml) water
½ cup (100g) sugar

Recipe Difficulty	Level 3
Prep. Time	20 min
Cook Time	60 min
Servings	1 cake
Wine	Champagne w/ red fruit taste

LETS GET STARTED...

1. Choose a shape for your cake and cut out a cardboard form to use on the bottom. First place the (decorated) part of the biscuit around the insides of the form and then a piece of biscuit on the bottom. Use a string to measure the length of the form before cutting the biscuit so it will fit as planned.

Red Fruit Mousse : **The next 2 steps need to happen at the same time.

2. A) Put ¾ cup (200ml) water in a pan and add ½ cup (100g) sugar. Dissolve slowly by heating. The sugar should be ready at 250 ºF (120 ºC). Without a temperature gage it should have a lot of big bubbles in the pan and look like a thick syrup.

3. B) Whisk the egg whites until thick in a mixer.

4. When both (A) & (B) steps are ready, add together in a mixer and continue mixing at a very low speed. Whisk the cream until thick (it is ready when you turn the bowl upside down and the cream doesn't move.)

5. Put the gelatin in cold water and remove when it's moist. In a blender, mush the strawberries until they achieve a fine texture. Add a little part of the strawberry mix with the gelatin and put over heat. When it has dissolved add back to the rest of the strawberry mix. Using a spatula, add the strawberry mix to the cream, by gently folding over itself. Next, stop mixing the first machine, and in the bowl, add the strawberry mix using a spatula. *Ensure the temperature of the mixture in the machine is room temperature maximum.

6. To finish: Pour the strawberry mousse into the form and place in the fridge for 2 hours. After 1 hour, remove from the fridge and spread strawberry jelly on top. Add red fruits or other decorative pieces you may have.

Did you know...

When your friends see this wonderful cake they will be very tempted to eat all of it. Your friends can try, unlike Tantalus. Tantalus stole the drink of a Greek God (a son of Zeus), shared it along with a secret of the gods with his people. He was caught and subsequently punished with eternal temptation. According to Greek legend, every time Tantalus reached for fruit the branches would raise. If he tried to drink the water, it would retreat away from him.

Strawberry Dessert Cake

TIPS AND TRICKS

When you cut the edges of the biscuit, cut diagonally and not straight. Joining the pieces of biscuit together this way hides the cut from your guests when you serve the cake. For variation, you can change strawberry to another red fruit but remember to also change the name of the cake!

PETIT FOUR

Petit four are generally considered small bite sized cakes or pastries, frequently served with tea or coffee at the end of the meal. They can be dry or sweet, with the possibilities so numerous some books are dedicated to just this area alone.

PETIT FOUR

You will learn how to complete some of these
petit four on the next few pages.

Sables Hollandaise

Mise en place

6 cups (750g) sifted flour
2¼ cup (500g) butter
2¼ cup (300g) powdered sugar, sifted
1 vanilla bean
½ zest lemon
Juice from ½ lemon
2 egg yolks
Flavour (e.g. cacao, coffee)

Recipe Difficulty	Level 2
Prep. Time	10 min
Cook Time	90 min
Servings	65 pieces
Wine	coffee or tea

Lets Get Started...

1. Mix the butter together with the flour. When you mix, don't make one big ball, mix trying to keep all the pieces of flour separate. Add the powdered sugar and continue to mix. When it has mixed well, cut the dough into two equal parts.

2. To the first dough add a flavour of your choice (e.g. cacao powder, coffee, zest) and mix.

3. To the second dough add the vanilla. To add the vanilla, cut the vanilla bean in two and scrape the black parts into the dough. Mix well.

4. Let the dough cool in the fridge a little. Once the dough has cooled, remove and roll the dough into rectangular shapes of the same size and once again, put back in the fridge to cool.

5. After the dough has sufficiently cooled, remove from the fridge and cut strips of the same size, in both pieces of dough right away. Use a ruler or form to aid in making the shapes the same size. Ideally you want the dough to be as cold as possible to make cutting the same size easier.

6. Arrange a strip of each type of dough together (light and dark) and then layer on top of each other. Using a brush, add a little water to help the dough's join together in the form you have cut it into. Use wax paper to push the pieces together instead of your hands. This helps to make sure that you don't heat or over handle the dough. Put back in the fridge to cool.

7. Cut thin slices (not too thin) and bake at 355 ºF (180 ºC) until brown.

Did you know...

Petit four is commonly served as a dish with coffee or tea after the meal. Cacao beans arrived in Europe after the travels of the Christopher Columbus to South America; however, Ethopia is most often credited for the creation of coffee. Initially, it was only kings and queens who began to enjoy this drink and it took nearly 200 years to become a common drink for the entire population. It is interesting to know that while the best coffee is sometimes considered Italian or Turkish, it actually originated from Ethopia.

Sables Hollandaise

TIPS AND TRICKS

Ensure the butter is mixed thoroughly in the dough when you start. This treat tastes very good regardless, but it is important to cut the strips the same size for appearance.

MACAROON

Mise en place

Circle piece with no teeth for the tip of the pastry bag

2½ cups (300g) (½ sugar, ½ almond powder) mixture
2 (60g) egg whites (a)
2 (60g) egg whites (b)

Filling for the macaroon
¼ lb (125g) fondant
9 tbsp (125g) butter

Recipe Difficulty	Level 3
Prep. Time	10 min
Cook Time	90 min
Servings	-
Wine	coffee or tea

LETS GET STARTED...

**The first 2 steps need to happen at the same time.

1. Put water in a pan and add sugar. Dissolve slowly by heating, the sugar will be ready at 250 °F (120 °C). If you do not have a temperature gauge it should look like a lot of big bubbles and syrupy.

2. Beat the egg whites (a) using a machine until thick.

3. When both steps are ready, continue to whisk in a mixer and add the sugar (slowly) from step 1. Keep beating for 15 minutes at a very slow speed.

4. In a second bowl, mix the other egg whites (b) with the ½ sugar, ½ almond powder mixture (called "tant pour tant").

5. Next gently fold the sugar and whites combined earlier into the "tant pour tant" mixture with a rubber spatula. Place this mixture into a pastry bag and drop ~ ¼ inch (3 cm) circles onto a non-stick baking sheet or use Silpats (see glossary). Bake 10 minutes or until they have a light brown color. Try not to overcook the macaroons or they will become dry.

Filling for the macaron (fondant & butter)

6. Whisk the fondant until it is soft. Then add the butter and keep whisking until you achieve a smooth texture. If desired, add flavouring such as coffee powder at this point. Once ready, put in a pastry bag and ready for use as the filling. Don't use for the macaroons filling until after they have finished baking and cooled to room temperature.

Did you know...

If you visit France, you will most likely consult the famous Michelin guide to restaurants to find a good place to eat. While most people say a restaurant has 1, 2, or 3 stars in the Michelin guide, they are actually not stars, they are "macarons."

Macaroon

PISTACHIO FRITTERS

Mise en place

Round tip for pastry bag
½ lb (210g) almond dough
1 tbsp (14g) pistachio dough
½ tbsp (11g) apricot marma-
lade
⅓ tbsp (8g) trimoline (optional)
Powdered sugar

2 (60g) eggs
1½ cup (30g) egg yolks
2½ tbsp (20g) flour
¼ cup cooled melted butter

Recipe Difficulty	Level 2
Prep. Time	10 min
Cook Time	45 min
Servings	20
Wine	Coffee or Tea

1. Preheat an oven to 425 ºF (220 ºC.)

2. First mix the almond dough, pistachio dough, marma-lade and trimoline in a bowl. Once thoroughly mixed, add the eggs, egg yolk, flour and dissolved butter in and mix.

3. When fully mixed, put this mixture into a pastry bag and drop in non-stick backing forms on a baking sheet.

4. Sprinkle powdered sugar over top using a sift. If you want a different taste, you can add pistachio, almond, or hazel-nuts. But first crush, and then sprinkle on top before baking.

5. Bake until form has set.

Pistachio Fritters

Did You Know...

While you eat this snack, called "Beignet Pistache" in French, you will notice that it contains pistachio which you find in the name of the dish. However, most people are at a loss to explain why it is called 'beignet'. If you know, we would love to hear your theory.

ALMOND TILE BISCUITS

Mise en place

3 tbsp (25g) powdered sugar
½ lb (250g) chopped almonds
½ cup +1 tbsp (70g) flour
2 pieces orange zest
¼ cup (50g) orange juice
⅔ cup (150g) melted butter

Recipe Difficulty	Level 1
Prep. Time	10 min
Cook Time	45 min
Servings	25
Wine	Coffee or tea

1. Preheat an oven to 390 ºF (200 ºC.)

2. Finely grind the almonds and mix with the powdered sugar in a large bowl. Add the flour, orange zest and the orange juice to this mixture. Add liquid butter until thoroughly mixed and put in the fridge.

3. When your dough is cold make small balls, approx. 2 tsp, put on the baking tray and bake at 390 ºF (200 ºC) until they achieve a brown color on the edges.

4. Remove them from the baking sheet carefully using a spatula and give them form by draping them over a shape that you like.

5. When they have cooled a little in the shape you desire, move to a wire rack to let them finish cooling.

Almond Tile Biscuits

Did You Know...

There is an expression in France 'avoir une tuile' which means that you have a problem. The saying originates from the old times when strong winds would blow a tile from its lodging and hit someone in the head while they walked down the street. Today the expression is used if someone has a problem. For this petit four, you should give the shape of this tile. To do this put it in a circle form after you remove it from the oven.

NOUGAT

Mise en place

2¼ cups (400g) sugar
½ cup (100g) liquid glucose preferred*
½ cup (100g) honey
4 (125g) egg whites
¾ lb (375g) sliced almonds
¼ lb (100g) chopped pistachios
⅛ lb (50g) finely chopped ginger
½ cup (100ml) water
a little powdered sugar

*substitute light corn syrup if necessary

Recipe Difficulty	Level 3
Prep. Time	10 min
Cook Time	60 min
Servings	4
Wine	Coffee or tea

LETS GET STARTED...

1. Put the honey, glucose (or light corn syrup), water, and sugar in a pan and cook to 310 ºF (156 ºC.)

2. Whisk the egg whites and then slowly add the sugar that was just cooked above inside. Make sure the egg whites and the sugar are ready at the same time as this is important for the success of that step.

3. After mixed, add in the almond and pistachio ingredients. Continue to whisk at a very slow speed for 15 minutes.

4. Roll out a leaf of wax paper coated with powdered sugar. Place two long iron pieces on each side to keep the nougat in place. You can also use a deep baking pan if desired.

5. When you have finished mixing the ingredients, pour your nougat mixture in the middle of the pan (or the irons), on top of the powdered sugar. Use a spatula to spread flat.

6. When the nougat has cooled you can cut and serve.

Did you know...

The candies/sweets in France are usually typical of one region. For example, the betises from Cambrai, and bouillabaisse from Marseilles. The nougat is a specialty of Montelimar, which is a town located in the Drome region near Valence. You can find three types of nougat; soft, medium, and hard. This recipe would be placed in the soft category.

Nougat

BASICS

This section includes some important basics you may want to familiarize yourself with. It starts out with basic repices and ends up wiht a glossary of useful terms.

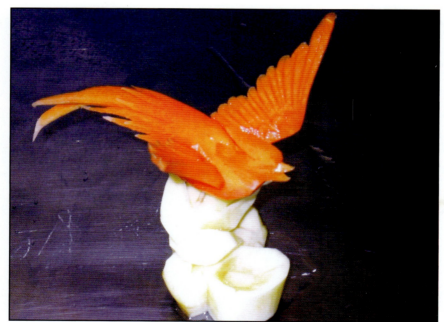

A "not so basic" carving made from a carrot & turnip

COURT BOUILLON

Mise en place

½ cup (100g) white vinegar
⅛ cup (30g) coarse Salt
⅔ lb (300g) carrot
½ lb (250g) onion
1 sprig thyme & bay leaf
10 cups (2.5 Litres) of water
Bouquet garnie

Recipe Difficulty	Level 1
Prep. Time	10 min
Cook Time	30 min

1. Wash and peel the carrots and onion, then slice emincer. If you are going to cook for a long time it is not necessary to slice very thin. Note that if you plan to eat the vegetables after cooking, cut them with a nice form so that they will look good on the plate. To give the carrots a different look, use a candeleur to make grooves down the sides before you cut.

2. Sweat the vegetables in the pot but don't let them change color.

3. Add water, the bouquet garnie, white wine, salt and pepper, and white vinegar in the pot and bring to a boil. After boiling, reduce heat and continue to simmer for minimum 10 minutes.

4. Strain if you do not want to keep or use the vegetables.

Court Bouillon

WHITE BUTTER

Mise en place

5 tbsp shallots
2½ tbsp white vinegar
2½ tbsp pepper
½ cup (125ml) white wine
3½ fl. oz (100ml) heavy cream
1 cup (250g) butter cubed

Recipe Difficulty	Level 1
Time	15 min
Quantity	¾ cup (150g) butter

1. Add just enough white vinegar to cover the bottom of a pan and heat. Add shallots and pepper and cook until almost all the vinegar is gone. Add white wine and cook until almost all liquid disappears. Add a little cream and boil, which helps thicken the sauce.

2. Add cold butter and swirl.

3. The recipe at this point, is simple and very good. If you have no other sauce to use with a fish, this recipe would be good. If you need ideas for a new sauce, add lemon, chives, curry, or flavors you enjoy to this recipe, the end result is usually very good. When you add these flavors name the sauce differently reflecting the ingredient you have added.

Step one

White Butter Finished

TIPS AND TRICKS

If you decide to add additional spice or flavor to this recipe it is best to do so when you add the white wine. However, if you decide to add herbs, it is better to add these after the butter.

BISCUIT

Mise en place

Biscuit
¼ lb (100g) of ½ sugar ½ almond powder mixture (sifted)
1 extra large (70g) egg
3 (100g) egg whites
2 tbsp. (25g) sugar, sifted
¾ tbsp (10g) dissolved butter
2 tbsp (15g) sifted flour

Rayure Cacao
⅛ cup (25g) butter
2½ tbsp (20g) sifted flour
2 tbsp (25g) sugar, sifted
1 (30g) egg white
*cacao powder for color

Recipe Difficulty	Level 1
Prep. Time	15 min
Cook Time	30 min

1. **Rayure Cacao:** Dissolve butter and whisk together in a bowl with sugar, egg white, and flour. Mix in the cacao and then spread smooth on a non-stick baking sheet (or use Silpats). Next you draw the design for the biscuit. Place in the fridge to let solidify a little before using with the biscuit.

2. **Biscuit:** Whisk ½ sugar, ½ almond powder mixture with the eggs until the texture is thick, and attains a cream color. Whisk egg white with the sugar until it becomes thick. *Add a tip of crème de tartare to make this easier or juice of lemon. Whisk slowly when you start to put the air inside, and add just a little sugar at the start to dissolve. When you start to see nice bubbles in the egg white you can start to whisk more quickly. Add the liquid butter to the mix of almond powder and eggs. Then using a spatula, add flour and mix by folding over itself. Using the same technique add a little of the egg white/sugar mix and continue to add until all is gone. Put in fridge with plastic wrap and let it rest for 10 minutes minimum.

3. Get the rayure cacao out of fridge and pour the biscuit over top (but not too thick). Put in oven at 355 ºF (180 ºC) until it achieves a golden color. This should be enough to be the base for a cake.

Removing the paper

TIPS AND TRICKS

To remove the leaf of paper once your biscuit is cooked, put a new leaf of paper on top of the biscuit, turn it over, and put on the table. The second leaf of paper helps ensure the biscuit does not stick to the table and makes it much easier to remove the first paper.

PÂTE A PÂTE

Mise en place

1 cup (130g) sifted flour
¼ cup (65g) butter
1 fl. oz (30ml) water
¼ tbsp (3g) salt
½ (25g) egg

Recipe Difficulty	Level 1
Time	15 min
Quantity	½ lb (250g) dough

1. Dust some flour on the work area so that the dough will not stick (repeat as needed). Another tip to help keep the dough from sticking is to move the dough frequently while you work.

2. Cut butter into little cubes and then mix with flour using an open motion with your hands. Mix the butter and the flour together breaking large pieces of butter apart when you find them. Add salt, and add 90% of the egg. *Keep 10% of the egg for the end in case there is any flour that needs a little extra moisture. Now work into a dough / ball and as soon as it looks like good dough, stop. The less you work the better as this way the dough will not be too elastic. Add flour or water as you need to get the right dough consistency. Ensure there are no small pieces by folding all the sides into one large piece. Place in the fridge for 30 minutes minimum.

Preparing the dough

Pâte a Pâte in a form

TIPS AND TRICKS

You can use this dough for pastries, or a salty dish like keish. You can keep the dough 2 or 3 days in the fridge by adding one or two drops of vinegar to keep it white.

PÂTE SUCRÉE

Mise en place

¾ cup (90g) sifted flour
½ cup (50g) sifted powder sugar
5 tbsp (70g) soft butter
2g salt, ½ vanilla bean
2½ tbsp (20g) sifted almond powder
1 (20g) egg yolk
*working flour

Recipe Difficulty	Level 1
Time	15 min
Quantity	½ lb (250g) dough

1. Dust some flour on the work area so that the dough will not stick (repeat as needed). Another tip to help keep the dough from sticking is to move the dough frequently while you work.

2. To make the butter soft, place in a bowl and pound with the end of a rolling pin or something similar. Wisk the butter into ¼ cup (30g) of the flour, then add salt, powder sugar, vanilla, egg yolk, and almond powder.

3. Put this dough in the middle and add the remainder of the flour around the outside. At this point you will have to mix (not whisk) with a spatula. Add a sprinkle of baking powder. Put in the fridge for 1 hour minimum.

TIPS AND TRICKS

It is better to work the dough minimally. The more you work it, the more the chemical reactions create gluten, which is what makes the dough hard and elastic later.

Pâte Sucrée

Did you know

The word "Pate" is given to any dough that can be transformed into a specific shape; the name "patisserie" for those working in the profession. Blessed with skills of precision and a great knowledge of fire, the patisseries took Saint Michel as their patron saint. Saint Michel is easily recognizable as he has one scale on his hand for measurement (precision) and a dragon at his feet to show he is a master of fire.

PÂTE BRISÉE

Mise en place

2 cups (250g) sifted flour
9½ tbsp. (135g) butter cubed
1½ tbsp (12.5g) powdered sugar sifted
½ tsp (2g) salt
1 egg

Recipe Difficulty	Level 1
Quantity	~1 lbs (450g) dough

1. Dust some flour on the work area so that the dough will not stick. Repeat this step as often as required. Another good idea to keep the dough from sticking is to move the dough frequently while you work.

2. Cut butter into little cubes and then mix with flour using an open motion with your hands. Said another way, you don't want to make a ball of dough with all the little pieces so try to never press the ingredients together. Break large pieces of butter apart when you find them. Mix the butter and the flour together with the powdered sugar and salt. Mix the water, egg white and egg yolk together and then add to the mixture. Try not to overwork the dough when you are adding the water. Refrigerate when done.

HEAD WAITER BUTTER

Mise en place

454g butter
juice from ½ lemon (more if desired for taste)
¼ cup (50g) finely chopped chives
(othet head waiter butters use parsley)
1 tbsp. salt
white pepper & shallots for taste

Recipe Difficulty	Level 1
Quantity	~1lb (454g) butter

1. In a bowl by hand, or using a blender, cream butter by beating slowly. Once the butter is smooth, add the other ingredients until fully mixed.

PÂTE FEUILLETÉE

Mise en place

4 cups (500g) flour
½ cup (125g) butter (small cubes)
½ tbsp (10g) salt
1¼ fl oz (37ml) white vinegar
¾ cup (190ml) water
1½ cups (375g) butter for stage 2

Recipe Difficulty	Level 2
Quantity	~2¾ lbs (1.2kg) dough

1. General ingredient information: The butter stops water from rising and breaking the pastry. By adding water into the first mix it helps solve this problem however the butter needs to be mixed evenly throughout. The white vinegar helps keep the flour and water from discoloring.

2. Steps: Cut butter into little cubes and then mix with flour and salt using an open motion with your hands. Said another way, you don't want to make a ball of dough with all the little pieces so try to never press the ingredients together. Break large pieces of butter apart when you find them. Premix the water and vinegar and then add to the dough and mix using your hands.

3. When finished make a ball with the dough and cut a cross in middle about ½ way through the dough. The purpose is to create easier use of the 4 leaves for stage 2 of the process. Place in the fridge (wrapped) for 10 min/20min to cool the dough and butter. Check it's not too soft with finger test, the dough should bounce back a little.

4. Stage 2: Soften the butter so that it will have a similar texture as the dough when it comes out of the fridge. To soften the butter use a rolling pin and hammer softly to soften. The method you choose depends on the hardness of the butter. Use a spatula to move in order to keep the butter from sticking to the bottom. Be careful to watch when it starts to get soft because it softens very quickly. Once at the right consistency make a small square/cube and prepare dough.

5. Always put an open end to your right as you need to turn to the same place each time you roll. Roll out 4 leaves of dough into square sections, it should look like a square cross with a high lump of dough in the middle. In the end it needs to be square so use your hands to fix if necessary. Put butter in middle where approx. ½ of the dough remains, then close leafs of dough in rotational pattern (i.e. North, West, South, East, do not close in a North-South-East-West pattern). Ensure to do this for consistency and to make the dough even and form throughout.

6. Keeping the open part to the right, working quickly overall, but while rolling the dough go very slowly because the butter needs this. Use even strength and roll in a north-south, east-west pattern. Roll in to a rectangular shape and when square fold the ends into the middle and then turn the end to right. Repeat the process and then put in fridge for 10min to allow the butter to cool. The total process requires 3 cycles, or a total of 6 turns. Note that you need to move it from the fridge quickly, and work quickly as the dough gets soft very quickly which will cause it to stick or break and ruin the pastry.

Fish Preparation

You need to be careful if you try to clean and prepare your own fish instead of buying filets. You should only attempt if you have had some experience and can complete safely, only you can judge this.

Cleaning: Cut away any fins on the fish using heavy scissors. Next remove scales by scraping the outside of the fish. When you do this step, scrape the fish inside a bag as the scales are very bad for drains and difficult to clean up. Cut along the bottom of the fish and remove any organs, blood or fat that you find. If you find blood deep inside the stomach of the fish, scrape away using a spoon and rinse under cold water. Remove the gills by cutting (or pulling) them out. Also remove any blood you find near the area.

Removing Scales

Filleting: Put the knife just behind (under) the gills and cut around the base of the head in a sawing type motion towards the bone. When you touch the bones stop cutting. Note for the first recipe in this section you would not cut around the head fully as you want to keep the head attached.

With the stomach of the fish to you, cut into the top of the fish (beside the fin). Cut until you find the backbone and then with the tip of the knife run along the length of the bones to cut away the filet. Ensure that you can always hear the knife along the bones when you cut, if you can't hear them stop because it means you are cutting inside the filet.

Start of Filet Process

Continue slowly to cut the fillet away from the fish bones, going all the way from the head to the tail. When you are finished, there should be some stomach skin still attached, cut this away and remove the fillet. Turn and repeat this technique on the other side of the fish and you are ready to cook. If you have a flat fish like Turbot use the same technique but remember there are 4 filets.

Tips: There are 2 sets of fish bones that you will find in a fish, the first you remove when you do your filet, the second is in the middle of that filet. To have a more enjoyable eating experience, remove all of these bones found in the filet using tweezers.

Seperating the filet from bones

CHICKEN PREPARATION

You need to be careful if you try to clean and prepare you own chicken instead of buying ready to cook. Only you can judge if you are able to complete these steps safely. Ensure that any equipment that has come in contact with raw chicken is washed well before using it for other ingredients or food.

Cleaning: Ensure that the internal organs (e.g. liver, stomach etc.) have been removed from the chicken as well as any unnecessary fat.

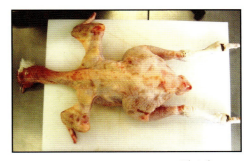
Chicken

If you are ready to roast: Have the chicken ready with the stuffing (if any) you desire. Prepare a skewer with a string through the end (like a thread & needle). Raise or lift the legs a little and push the skewer through the chicken just behind the legs. Tuck the wings under the chicken and then push the skewer through the big wing first, then through the neck skin (which you have pulled up to close the hole), then through wings on other side. Pull the string through, spin to keep in place and tie once. With a hand on the side of chicken, use a little force and push on the breastbone to break and separate a little. Tie the string two more times and cut away any excess. To finish we need to close the last cavity. Take the skewer and go under the feet, through skin at the back, over feet and through the skin once again to close the back of the chicken.

Prep for Roasting

Removing the filets: With the legs of the chicken down, cut the back lengthwise then across in the shape of a cross on back. Stop cutting where the legs of the chicken start. Turn the chicken over, and start to cut the legs away from the chicken. Cut the skin between the breast and leg towards the cross and stop there. Cut only the skin not the meat. When you cut away the legs, try to capture a good piece of meat called the "oyster", there are two of them located on the back by the thigh joint. Break the leg backwards so that it separates from the joint, pull and then remove by cutting with the knife. Repeat for the second leg. Next, cut right down the side of back bone towards the front of the chicken to start the breast. When you reach the wishbone at the front, stop and slide your knife along this bone towards the wings. When you get to the bottom right by the wing, chop to remove. If you do this correctly it will cut the breast out nicely. To cut bones always try to use diagonal cuts not square as square will fragment the bone.

Chicken filet pieces

VEGETABLE CUTS

Turn cut zucchini - Anglais

Turn cut carrot & turnip - Glaze

Boquet Garnie

Monder

Julienne (1mm thick)

Zuchini prep for 'turn' cut

Ciseler (chalots)

Julienne (1mm thick)

Emincer - cut top & peel, use fine slice and cut with grain

VISUALIZED

Baked tomato skins from monder -
good garnish, ok taste

concasse de tomate

Brunoise -
macedoine (5mm)

chifonade -lettuce

Brunoise -
gross (2/3mm)

Jardiniere -
5mm, 6/7cm long

Brunoise -
fine (1mm)

Paysanne - always
triangle shape,
always same size
of vegetables

GLOSSARY

Aerate: adding air into an ingredient making it lighter with an increased volume.

Anglaise (vegetables): add a good amount of salt to a pot of water and bring to a boil. When the water is boiling, add the vegetables and cook. Immediately after the vegetables are ready, remove and put in cold water with ice (ice helps keep color in vegetable and stops the cooking process).

Bain Marie: put the bowl with the contents on top and inside of another pot that has boiling water to allow it to cook indirectly.

Baste: Spooning juices over an ingredient to help keep moist.

Bouquet Garnie: is a bundle of seasonings used in cooking for flavour, typically with stocks. The size of the bouquet garnie should equal the cooking time (for longer cook times use a bigger bouquet.)

Wash a leek, and cut the leaves at the base (near the roots) so that you have a ~3 inches/ 6/7cm length. Ensure the leaves of the leek are clean, put 1 sprig thyme and bay leaf inside a leek leaf, and then cover with other leaves to close. Tie 3 times on each end with string. If you want to add pepper, add it to the middle and ensure to fold closed the leaves containing the pepper on the ends so that it doesn't fall out.

Braised: Braisè in French, means to cook covered in a small amount of liquid for an extended period of time.

Broiling: is cooking one side of a dish on very high heat using radiant heat. A low intensity broiler sometimes referred to is a salamander.

Brunoise: There are 3 different types of 'Brunoise' that are distinctive by size:

Fine	1mm	
Grosse	2-3mm	⅛ inch
Macedoine	5mm	¼ inch

Using a mandolin, cut thin slices of the vegetables and put flat on a table. Layer the left edge of vegetables over the right (so that they don't move when you cut), cut thin slices lengthwise first to the thickness desired (above). When finished with the first cut turn and repeat small cuts finishing the cubes.

Ciseler : is the name of the technique to finely mince onions and shallots. First cut away the shallots roots and peel. Take the roots and place them away from you. Cut 80% along the grain.

Note you don't cut all the way through the top of the roots so that you can turn intact. Finish by cutting and creating very small cubes.

Chiffonade: is used for shredded leafy greens. Take a leafy vegetable or herb, and slice it almost julienne thin. The trick is to roll the leaf like a cigar shape. If you do it right, the leaf will not crack, and when cut it will keep its color longer.

Concasse de Tomate / Tomato Concasse: refers to making tomato cubes after you remove the skin (see "monder"). Cut the tomato width-wise not length wise so you can remove the seeds. Using your fingers, remove the seeds. Then do one cut émincer and then cut ciseler. Take shallots or onions cut ciseler, add garlic chopped, with olive oil, sugar, salt, pepper, thyme and a little bay leaf. Cook until all the water is gone.

It is also possible for a recipe to list uncooked tomato concasse. In this case, only perform the technique of skinning, seeding, and cubing.

Confit: is cooking meat slowly in its own fat, with seasonings, vegetables and/or wine until tender.

Cornet: are small paper cones used for decorating. They have smaller openings than pastry bag tips which can make them better for very fine lines when writing or decorating cakes and pastries.

Crustacean: a term used to describe animals usually elongated and enclosed in a hard shell such as lobsters, crabs, shrimp and crayfish. It is a sub group of the larger group called shellfish.

Duxelle: Mushroom mixture, peel mushrooms and remove black parts. Slice very fine from the top and stop when black of ring starts to show. Cut julienne and then fine brunoise. Melt oil and butter in hot pan (no color though), add mushrooms first and cook, then add shallots, s&p. Don't move around too much or temperature of the pan will drop and the mushrooms will boil. When color achieved it is cooked, add white wine and do reduction Add cream and do emulsification.

Émincer: a technique that means to cut into thin slices, used often with carrots and onions. Try to keep the size of the slices very fine for width. Cut the vegetables in halves or fours so that they are not too big when you are finished.

Emulsify: Typically means to combine two ingredients that are difficult to put together, sometimes with the use of an extra ingredient (e.g. butter, mustard.)

Glacer: means to glaze. Add water to a level equal with the vegetables and bring slowly to boil. Add butter, sugar, salts and water to a pan. Use just enough sugar and salt to just cover the vegetables. Add vegetables to the mixture and cover the pan with wax paper with a hold cut in the middle and saute.

Hacher: means to chop. There are no set guidelines for this technique but the goal is to have very small pieces of what you are chopping when finished.

Hors d'Oeuvres: are small dishes typically served at a party or at the start of a meal. Canapè is an example of these found at the start of the book.

Jardinière: is usually seen as mixed diced vegetables. The cuts should be about ¼ inch / 5mm thick and ~3 inches/ 6-7cm length. When finished they have a shape similar to a french fry.

Julienne: vegetables that are very finely sliced and used primarily for garnish. First cut vegetables an equal length, preferably ~3 inches/ 6/7cm. Next use the mandolin to cut those vegetables into very thin (1mm), flat pieces. To finish, place flat on the table and cut very thin slices.

If you are doing a leek julienne remove the middle (core) part as it is hard and difficult to use.

Langouste: Spiny or rock lobsters a sub family of the crustaceans. Langoustines are smaller and often called rock shrimp.

Monder: is the technique used to remove the tomato skin. Cut the top stem out, and using a knife put a small 'x' on the bottom where the seam is. Put the tomato in boiling water for 10 sec. This is a sensitive measurement so note its ok to go to maybe 9 or 11 seconds, but at 20 sec. you will have problems. Use your thumb and knife to remove the skin starting where you made the 'x'. You should be able to complete in about 5 or 6 long strokes if the tomato has been in the water for the correct amount of time.

Pan Fry: cook over moderate heat in a moderate amount of fat.

Paysanne: typically means cut vegetables in a triangle shape. Today squares are also occasionally used for these recipes.

Poach: Pochè in French, poaching means to gently cook or simmer food in another liquid at approx. 170 °F (77 °C.)

Reduction: a technique used for sauces where over low heat (simmer), a liquid is cooked to reduce the volume but keep and intensify the flavour.

Roast: Rôti in French, roasting means cooking, uncovered using a dry heat source. Most often this would be in the oven, but an open flame is also used.

Sauté: means to cook quickly in a short amount of time over high heat in a pan with a small amount of fat. Many times people will refer to "jumping" the food (flipping in the air.)

Silpat: is a non-stick sheet used for baking in many kitchens both professional and novice.

Simmer: is a technique where foods are cooked in other liquids at approx. 200 °F (90 °C.)

Sweat: sweating vegetables means to cook over low heat to make the vegetables 'sweat' and bring the flavour out into the sauce or liquid.

Tourner: "To turn", you may find this technique difficult to perfect. First you need to cut the vegetables the same length (~3 inches/6cm). Place your thumb and index finger of the hand not cutting on either end of the vegetable. Now place the knife next to your finger and bring it towards your thumb in the motion of an arc, like a rainbow. You are trying to round the vegetable so try to make even strokes in the shape of a rainbow. If you stop in the middle it will give an uneven look to the vegetable. Also important to note that if your knife is not very sharp it will make the smooth strokes very difficult to do well.

*Potato "vapeur" is a larger size cut (¼ lb) so do not cut in half before starting. You should make only 7 cuts to get to the end 'turn' cut potato.

**Zucchini is just shaping the top and cutting away the part not needed at bottom.

***Note that you don't need to peel the vegetables first because they are peeled when you cut.

Trou Normand: served after fish and before the meat it is a digestive used to cleanse the palate and enhance the appetite for the rest of the planned meal. In Normandy it was known as a shot of apple brandy, however today it is more often a sorbet with apple brandy. The time in between allows some time for digestion and the alcohol an effective tool to kill any bacteria.

COOKING CONVERSION TABLES

TEMPERATURE

Celsius	Farenheit
50	122
60	140
70	158
80	176
90	194
100	212
110	230
120	248
130	266
140	284
150	302
160	320
170	338
180	356
190	374
200	392
210	410
220	428
230	446
240	464
250	482

VOLUME

tbsp	cups	ml	fl. oz
1	-	15	0.5
4	¼	60	2
8	½	120	4
12	¾	180	6
16	1	240	8
32	2	480	15.4
33	2.1	495	16
64	4	960	31

WEIGHT

gr	lbs	oz
56	⅛	2.0
113	¼	4.0
150	⅓	5.3
227	½	8.0
300	⅔	10.5
340	¾	12.0
454	1	16.0

SPECIFIC INGREDIENT CONVERSIONS USED

	cups	*gr	ml	fl. oz
Cream (heavy)	½	125	125	4.2
Milk	½	125	120	4.1
Olive Oil	½	110	120	3.7
Syrup	½	185	135	-
Vinegar	½	125	125	4.2
Wine	½	125	125	4.2
Water	½	125	125	4.0

	lbs	*gr	cups	tbsp
Butter (unsalted)	¼	113	½	8
Cheese (grated)	¼	110	1	-
Flour	¼	125	1	16
Salt (regular)	⅓	150	½	8
Sugar	¼	115	⅝	9½
Sugar (powdered)	¼	125	1	16

	lbs	*gr	cups	ea
Carrot	¼	125	1	2
Cucumber/Zuchini	⅓	150	1	½
Leek	¼	120	1⅓	1⅓
Mushrooms (sliced)	¼	125	1¾	7
Onion	¼	110	¾	1
Potato (baking)	¼	113	1½	½
Red berries (whole)	¼	125	1	
Shallots (diced)	¼	120	¾	2½ (12 tbsp)
Sweet Bell Pepper	¼	120	¾	1
Tomato	¼	125	⅔	1

*grams were the basis for all ingredients in all recipes and you should weigh all ingredients for the best results. 113.5g = ¼lb, the conversions used were to the #grams above and chosen for convenience to cups, or tbsp, or ea to help you. Fruits and vegetables are medium sized, cups chopped/diced unless noted, almonds converted to 1 cup, sliced and chopped at 85g

INDEX